The
Challenge
of the
Apocalypse

Embracing the
Book of Revelation
with
Hope and Faith

The
Challenge
of the
Apocalypse

Embracing the
Book of Revelation
with
Hope and Faith

LAURIN J. WENIG

PAULIST PRESS
New York/Mahwah, N.J.

Scripture quotations are taken from the New Revised Standard Version Bible (NRSV), © 1989 by the Division of Christian Education of the National Council of the Churches of Christ in the United States of America, and are used by permission.

Artwork in this text is from the series of woodcuts by the German artist Albrecht Dürer on themes from the Book of Revelation. These works first appeared in print in 1498.

The maps are from the Paulist Press collection, donated as a courtesy by the author.

Cover and interior design by Lynn Else

Library of Congress Cataloging-in-Publication Data

Wenig, Laurin.
    The challenge of the apocalypse : embracing the book of Revelation
    with hope and faith / by Laurin J. Wenig.
        p. cm.
    Includes bibliographical references and index.
    ISBN 0-8091-4064-0 (alk. paper)
    1. Bible. N.T. Revelation—Texbooks. I. Title.

BS2825.55 .W46 2002
228'.044—dc21

2001058790

Published by
PAULIST PRESS
997 Macarthur Boulevard
Mahwah, New Jersey 07430

www.paulistpress.com

Printed and bound in the United States of America

CONTENTS

FOREWORD

Christians have been thinking about the end of the world ever since the beginning. They have wondered when the end of the world would come and what would happen when the world ended. They have particularly wondered, "What will happen to me?"

Everyone has seen the comical drawing of the wild man dressed in a white gown, standing on a soapbox on a street corner holding a placard that reads "Repent! The end is near!" Although we tend to satirize our fears about the end of the world, the Scriptures and our faith make us take this uncomfortable and fascinating topic quite seriously. In our Creed we confess that we believe "in the life of the world to come." In the Our Father we pray "Thy kingdom come." Just what are we praying for? How are we to understand these words and the faith they express? What does the Bible tell us about the end of the world?

The purpose of this little book is to help us see one of the ways that the Bible invites us to wait for the end of the world. It invites us to see the response made by the early Christians. To be sure, the Book of Revelation is not the only response. Nor is this book the final interpretation of the Book of Revelation. In our lives we wait for many things. We wait to grow up. We wait to graduate from school. We wait to find the right job. We wait to meet the right partner for marriage. During all this time, we are also waiting for God.

How should we wait? We all seek a way to God and the kingdom. All of these types of waiting fall into one of two general types. One way is to sit back and wait for the final judgment, when Jesus will come riding on a cloud to separate the sheep from the goats, the good people from the evil people, to welcome us into his Father's kingdom or to deliver us into the depths of hell. The second option is to get involved in the affairs of history, to discern that there is a personal and ecclesial role in shaping and fashioning the future of my own life, my community, and the world in which I live.

One of the ways of waiting is to wait in fear and dread expectation of the future. The other way is to wait in hope. In a sentence, one of the most important decisions a Christian can make is how to think about the end of his or her life.

In traditional Christian theology, the end time or eschaton involved four aspects: death, judgment, heaven, hell. The attitude that we choose about the ultimate purpose of life and our beliefs about life after death will condition our entire lifestyle. For a true Christian, meaningful life can only come from genuine effort to understand the gospel of Jesus. Meaningful (and fearless) living comes from having a strong faith in knowing where we came from (the Father) and where we are going (to the Father). Meaningful life, baptized living, cannot be preoccupied with dread of God, fear of other people, or fear of the future. Genuine Christian life is hopeful and positive. It is an outlook on the world and its potential as seen through the eyes of God. It is for this reason that a study of the last things should really be one of the first items on a Christian's agenda.

In the pages that follow you will read about the future as expressed in the Bible, especially the Book of Revelation. Some of these passages were written in order to inspire serious thinking, even fear, in people. Others were written to reflect the hopes of the people of God in difficult and confusing times. Doesn't that sound familiar?

Some of the questions we will explore are:

1. Can we detect the Coming of the Lord?

2. When can we expect the Coming of the Lord?

3. What happens to Christians who die before the world ends?

4. How will the world end? with a whimper or a bang?

5. What information can we gain by reading the Scriptures?
   - Who are the false prophets?
   - What about the horrible judgments described in the Bible?

- How do we interpret the message of Revelation?

You are about to venture into a very exciting and controversial area of theological study. I urge you to keep your mind and soul open for some surprising detours along the path. A recommended approach to this study, either in groups or individually, would be to read carefully the biblical passages under consideration; second, read the text of this guide; then reread the biblical passages and take some time to ponder the questions for reflection.

As the twenty-first century begins, everyone is wondering what will happen. Will something special occur? How should we look at this turning of the calendar? With secular eyes? With what religious insights? One purpose of this book is to help people place the Book of Revelation in the context of faith and hope, the context of the Church, rather than to be swayed and made fearful by the inevitable proclamations and interpretations that always come forward as the clock ticks away toward the future.

In a world that sometimes seems to have gone so awry, the Christian ought to stand out as a person of hope. The Christian is the person who understands that the dying and rising of everyday life, and the trials and errors of human existence, all lead to a future. The future is the hope of a common humanity, a blessed community where the Word of God is lived fully and joyfully. It is that Word that you will explore in this book. It is the Word of faith, the Word of hope, and the Word of charity, the revelation of God to us through the Son, the Risen Christ, our Lord and Brother.

Rev. Laurin J. Wenig

Chapter 1

The Strange Nature of the Book of Revelation

I. Introduction

Apocalyptic literature can be understood only if we have a firm grasp of its terminology and form. *Apocalyptic* means "to uncover" or "to reveal." An apocalypse could be called "a revelation of what God intends to do at some time in the future."

The term *eschatology* refers to the last things. Eschatology deals with the "eschaton"—the final age toward which the world, history, and time are moving. Generally, eschatological notions involve the cooperation between God and humankind in bringing about the final age. Apocalyptic, on the other hand, stresses the sudden inbreaking of God's rule that will definitely establish the kingdom. It is beyond human control. That inbreaking is the "end of the world" in the usual sense of that phrase.

There are many different theological opinions about the nature of the eschaton and how God works through history. None of them have been able to capture 100 percent agreement among theologians throughout the ages. In fact, perhaps the best way to understand them is to see how each of them contains its own form of truth. By balancing them against one another we get the best overview. None is totally correct; none is totally wrong. The biblical writers, for various reasons, present this variety of approaches to us. One author leans in one direction; another leans in the opposite direction. It is best to understand that this controversy shouldn't upset us. It has always been there. Rather than seeing it as a problem it can be viewed as part of the rich diversity of the expressions of faith that we find in the Scriptures.

The first viewpoint is *consistent eschatology*. It is based on the end-of-the-world expectations that were popular during the first century. Jesus' first words in the Gospel of Mark are "The time is fulfilled, and the kingdom of God has come near; repent, and believe in the good news" (Mark 1:15). Theologians who adhere to this school say that these kinds of words from Jesus indicate that he, like many others at the time, expected that the end of the world was near. The actions and preaching of Jesus were aimed at inaugurating that end time during his life on earth.

The second viewpoint is *realized eschatology*. This is the idea that the end time has already happened and is already present to us. The end time took place in the person of Jesus. Jesus is the full revelation of the Father. This is especially the way the end time is presented in the

Gospel of John. It is the duty of Christians to live a lifestyle that reflects the "already" nature of God's kingdom in our lives.

The third viewpoint is *salvation-history eschatology*. This outlook is probably the most representative school for people, especially Catholics. It is sort of a combination of the consistent and realized eschatological outlooks. Often it is summarized as the "already-but-not-yet" school This means that at any given time in history the people of God find themselves somewhere between creation (the beginning) and the end of the world. In this meantime/in-between time, we are able to hear the gospel, to believe it, and to live with faith and hope. Our faithful witnessing and activity will help to bring about the end of the world.

You might picture it like this:

CREATION
the beginning of time

JESUS
initiates end of time

CHURCH
lives in the present
moment of time

PAROUSIA
full establishment of
the kingdom at the
end of time

The fourth form of eschatological thinking is *dialectical eschatology,* or *apocalyptic.* This school believes that the end of the world will come about through a great inbreaking from above. It will be God's intervention in history at some unknown future moment. It is radically orientated toward futurist theologies and philosophies. It is, as the name might indicate, a chief characteristic of the Book of Revelation.

II. Characteristics of Apocalyptic Literature

The German theologian Klaus Koch* writes that there are six characteristics that help us to identify a piece of writing as apocalyptic. If we find most of these characteristics grouped together in a single piece of literature, it can be considered apocalyptic. These characteristics are:

1. Great Discourse Cycles: These sections show the author discussing the meaning of events, especially future events, with an interpreter. Often this interpreter is an angel or some kind of heavenly messenger. For example:

I was in the spirit on the Lord's day, and I heard behind me a loud voice like a trumpet saying, "Write in a book what you see and send it to the seven churches."... Then I turned to see whose voice it was that spoke to me, and on turning I saw seven golden lampstands, and in the midst of the lampstands I saw one like the Son of Man, clothed with a long robe and with a golden sash across his chest (Rev 1:10–12).

---

*Klaus Koch, *The Rediscovery of Apocalyptic Studies in Biblical Theology,* 22 (Naperville: Alex N. Allenson, Inc., 1970) 24–28.

2. Description of the Vision of the Author: In these passages the author uses a stereotyped style of reporting the psychological effect of what has been seen or heard. For example, "When I saw him, I fell at his feet as though dead" (Rev 1:17). One cannot hear such words without a personal, often physical response to them.

3. Content of the Message: The dreams and visions of the author serve to give a community that is undergoing trial or persecution some sense of hope that it has not been abandoned by God. Often the authors will reach back into history to narrate tales of the way past generations were saved from dreadful circumstances because they continued to hope in the power of God to save them. The Book of Daniel is a good example. Often these messages are written in a kind of code language. The language is deliberately obscure so that it would be understood only by the audience for whom it was intended. Our own difficulties in understanding the Book of Revelation stem from the obscurity of this code language. The great signs and symbols were meant to offer hope and to open up the future actions of God in order to give strength to a people in distress. By this sort of literature people might be released from their psychological or spiritual sufferings.

4. Pseudonymity: The pseudonymity of apocalyptic writings had two purposes. First, often the name ascribed to the author was the name of a famous person from the past. This lent prestige to the work and made it a more

saleable and believable item. It would be as though a contemporary author would use the name of William
Shakespeare instead of his or her own name. The second
reason for pseudonymity was to make a stronger impact
on the audience. If the author could show that he had fulfilled prophecies that were made long ago, it gave a
stronger base of hope to the audience. The Book of
Revelation is an exception to this norm because the author
constantly repeats the fact that he is the seer to whom the
visions are being revealed.

5. Mythical Imagery: The delight of reading apocalyptic literature is its rich use of symbolism. It is the same
rich symbolism that confuses us in our attempts to interpret
it. Bizarre images, awesome beasts, the symbolic use of
numbers (7, 12, 40, 666), the word-portraits that use surre-
alistic color tones are all elements of the special nature of
the apocalyptic genre. Daniel tells us, "After this, as I
watched, another appeared, like a leopard. The beast had
four wings of a bird on its back and four heads; and dominion was given to it" (Dan 7:6). The colors represent certain
characteristics, just as the black hat and white hat in a modern cowboy movie are clues to the characters of the wear-
ers. White demonstrates joy and victory. Black is the color
of death. Red is the color of blood. Purple is the color of
royalty and the luxuries that accompany a royal personage.

6. Composite Character: Often apocalyptic literature seems disjointed. The sections of the book indicate

that it came from a number of sources that were compiled by the author and woven together for a single purpose. Sometimes one person in the narrative represents several characters or problems. For examples of these characteristics, which are common in the Book of Revelation, read the Book of Daniel, Mark 13, or Matthew 24.

III. The Apocalyptic Outlook on Life

The Germans call it *Weltanschauung*. Translated, it means "worldview." The term encompasses the whole set of presuppositions that any society or individual has and lives with every day regarding the world. That includes such things as the mores, culture, science, and fabric of daily existence of a people at any given time. It means that the way we look at our individual roles in the world, as well as our community role in the world, has a great influence on our behavior and attitudes as individuals and as a society. A worldview can move a society toward progress and development or toward stagnation and decay. Worldviews of societies can be positive or negative. Perhaps one very broad analogy that might explain how outlooks can affect the everyday lives of a people would be to compare the worldview of capitalism to that of communism. These are two radically different ways of life, based upon philosophies and economic theories that touch the daily existence of millions of people.

Another example is that of ancient Egypt. For them, it was important that every day be like the one before it, that every year duplicate the one that preceded it. This cyclic view of life was guaranteed by the annual flooding of the Nile, harvest, planting, flooding of the Nile, harvest, planting, and so on. All worship was orientated toward guaranteeing the continual order of this cycle. It affected Egypt's outlook on the purpose of the world, history, the role of leadership, and religion.

Two more examples are the old beliefs that the world was flat or that the earth was the center of the universe. These worldviews affected theology, science, and philosophy for hundreds of years.

In every era of history there have been worldviews. Often the worldview of one group is in conflict with that of another. Sometimes they coexist. Usually they do not.

In biblical times, from approximately 200 B.C.E until 200 C.E., people were preoccupied with the worldview we now term "apocalyptic." This meant that for most people the situation of life had become so desperate that it seemed there was little that a person or group could do to better their situation or to eliminate their oppressors. Five hundred years prior to the beginning of apocalyptic literature, the prophets of Israel had encouraged people to participate actively in their society. The world was given to people to conquer and to develop. All this could be done if only

Israel would be faithful to its covenant with Yahweh. The prophets uttered a call to action to their peers.

Apocalyptic writers did just the opposite. For them, only God could be in control of a world and history that had gone wrong. Human effort against the overwhelming evils of the day was futile. Instead of a call to action, as the prophets had uttered, people were encouraged to wait until God would finally act on their behalf. There was nothing they could do.

Although it seems somewhat simplistic, apocalypticists divide things into two camps, the "good guys and the bad guys." This approach toward a worldview is called dualism. One characteristic is to divide all of world history in two eras—that which is now and that which is to come. Everything falls neatly into these categories of good and evil, right and wrong, the reign of Satan and the reign of God. The entire cosmos is affected by these two fundamental realms of existence. Both claim our allegiance.

This kind of worldview originated in times of great distress for God's people. Some of the first smatterings of apocalyptic literature began as a response to the questions of the Exile. Because everything that had been part of Israel's life seemed to disappear, writings came about to give hope to the people that God was still in control. There is a good example of this in Isaiah 24–28. At a later time, when Greek cultural domination threatened to eliminate the faith traditions of Israel, parts of the Book of

Daniel were written in an apocalyptic fashion to give hope to a people who were in distress. In fact, from the time of the composition of the Book of Daniel until 200 years into the Christian Era, those who believed in Yahweh saw their lives in terms of affliction. If you can, imagine the kind of anguish those generations of people took for granted. "Who will overrun us next?" was their philosophy, their *Weltanschauung*. These suffering people needed hope, something to hang on to. The writings of the apocalyptic authors pointed toward signs that there was an end in sight to the sufferings of the present moment. The signs included visions of the future that told them that their tribulation would finally pass away. The seers in apocalyptic writings looked into the future and saw the end of earthly existence in terms of great cosmic catastrophes. Because human effort is useless, cosmic warfare is waged by angels. In the Book of Revelation, the power of God and the power of Satan do battle in the persons of Michael the Archangel, assisted by other angels, and a great dragon assisted by his "angels."

"And war broke out in heaven; Michael and his angels fought against the dragon. The dragon and his angels fought back, but they were defeated, and there was no longer any place for them in heaven. The great dragon was thrown down, that ancient serpent, who is called the Devil and Satan, the deceiver of the whole world — he was thrown down to the earth, and his angels were thrown down with him" (Rev 12:7–9).

IV. Conclusion

There have been many times in history when it seemed the world was about to end. Christians and Jews of the first century thought that the world was going to end when the Romans destroyed Jerusalem and the Temple in 70 C.E.

Later, around the year 1000 C.E., people again began to predict that the world would end as the time of the first millennium of Christianity approached. This outlook is called *millennialism*. In fact, with each advance in the technology of warfare, people were sure that the next war would mark the end of the world. In the twentieth century, people were certain the end was near because of the dreadful events of the Nazi Holocaust during World War II. The ever present threat of nuclear annihilation will undoubtedly continue to send ripples of apocalyptic thinking through the world. It is a valid worldview that is not limited to a long time ago. Apocalyptic writings and outlooks, like fashion styles, come and go in popularity.

For the believing Christian, however, the words of hope offered in the Book of Revelation ought to eliminate all fear:

"The one who testifies to these things says,
'Surely I am coming soon.' Amen. Come, Lord
Jesus!"

(Rev 22:20)

Questions for Reflection

1. What is the basic difference between eschatological viewpoints and apocalyptic viewpoints?

2. What are the four main eschatological theories?

3. Which theory seems to describe your thoughts about the end of the world?

4. How can there be so many opinions? Is this confusing or enriching?

5. Which theory best describes the views of our times?

6. What are the major characteristics of apocalyptic writings?

7. How would you describe your worldview? What elements of culture, religion, and expectation are part of it?

8. Which books, movies, or plays reflect the apocalyptic worldview in our society? How do they do this?

Chapter 2

Why the Book of Revelation Was Written

I. Introduction

Apocalyptic writing is very special. Authors used it to express their concerns and their hopes for the future of God's people. In the Old Testament, that was the people of Israel, the chosen people. In the New Testament the people of God are the church, that small community of people who came to believe that Jesus of Nazareth was the Messiah, the Son of God, who lived and died for them, who redeemed them, who rose from the dead, and who would come again.

The Christian church had its humble beginnings in Jerusalem. Archaeology shows that this community of believers, still very much Jewish in origin and background, had its headquarters on Mount Sion (Zion). To this day Christians carefully maintain the sites associated with the life of Jesus and the early church. In that location, on the southwest hill of the city of Jerusalem, the Cenacle marks the site of the Last Supper. The Dormition

Abbey is built over the site of the death of Mary and Pentecost. Already in the first centuries synagogue-churches were built for worshipers. The Byzantine era (312–614 C.E.) witnessed the construction of beautiful churches throughout the area. The Roman Emperor Constantine made that construction legal when he recognized Christianity as a religion of the realm. This happened when he issued the Edict of Milan in 312 C.E. Before that time Christianity was illegal. Its practitioners were outlaws and subject to punishment. Many early Christians paid this ultimate price for their faith.

That community that gathered on Mount Sion (Zion) knew difficulties. They were barely tolerated by mainline Jewish sects. Already by the end of the second decade of Christianity, they had begun to separate from their Jewish roots over the question of kosher laws and circumcision (Acts 15). It was a church, a group of believers, making decisions that would have much influence over the future. But in the meantime, those decisions caused much discussion and divisions as people took sides for one idea or another. In 66 C.E. that Christian community fled Jerusalem, anticipating the fall of the city at the hands of the Romans. (Jerusalem did fall to the Romans in 70 C.E.)

It was from Jerusalem that the earliest Christian missionaries went forth to proclaim their faith in Jesus. The Word went out and spread throughout the Mediterranean world until, by the end of the Acts of the Apostles, it could truly be said that the message of Jesus had been preached to all the ends of the earth. This was so because Paul, that energetic and eloquent spokesman, had reached the capital of the realm, Rome, and proclaimed Christ there. Like Peter, he would also give his life for his Lord in Rome, the political capital of the empire.

Much of Paul's missionary activity was centered in Turkey. In his letters and in the Acts of the Apostles we read a litany of familiar names: Troy, Ephesus, Galatia, Pergamum. He preached the gospel to people whose origins were Gentile, not Jewish. After they heard the gospel they came to believe in Jesus and were baptized. Some of these churches were filled with enthusiasm for their new-found salvation. Others were more cautious. But on those shores an early, enthusiastic, and dazzling Christianity was developing.

The more it developed, however, the more of a threat it became to the established religions of the Roman imperial state and of the local gods and goddesses, priests and priestesses. Persecutions, both physical and psychological, began to sweep over this territory. They originated in imperial Rome but reached throughout the empire. The result was a great deal of pain and uncertainty. Those who were weak yielded to the pressures. They gave up their new faith in the face of opposition. Others were wavering. What course of action should they follow?

In order to shore up their faith in these difficult times, John wrote the Book of Revelation. Anyone who has read it knows that it is out of the ordinary. In fact, it is bizarre. Its style and message are so out of line with the rest of the New Testament that it was almost not included in the Bible. That would have been a tragic loss. With a little concentration and a lot of reflection we can see that this book is a unique treasure. Its message was intended to address specific situations and times, but behind the symbolism, there is also a message for all time, as we will discover.

II. Authorship

"The revelation of Jesus Christ, which God gave him to show his servants what must soon take place; he made it known by sending his angel to his servant, John, who testified to the word of God and to the testimony of Jesus Christ, even to all that he saw" (Rev 1:1–2).

The introduction to Revelation mentions that the author is someone named John. Who is this John? For centuries people assumed that this John was surely the same John whose name is associated with the Fourth Gospel. The John of the Book of Revelation tells us that he is a fellow sufferer in the difficult situation of the times: "I, John, your brother who share with you in Jesus the persecution and the kingdom and the patient endurance, was on the island called Patmos because of the word of God and the testimony of Jesus" (Rev 1:9).

We learn here that this John knew the problems of the times well. He was part of the people who were bearing the pains and the uncertainties of the era. He looks very much like a prophet—one who proclaims God's Word. Like the Old Testament prophets, his reward for his efforts is persecution and trouble. He now finds himself in exile on the island of Patmos. He also calls himself a servant (v. 1). That's all he tells us on his own.

Is this the same John who wrote the Gospel? Scholars disagree on exactly who he was, but most modern scholars agree that the John who wrote this message is probably not the same as the author of the Gospel, even though they share the same name. Why?

First, there is a language problem. The original Greek text of the Gospel of John is well written. It reveals an author who knew the language well and could express himself with some skill. The style of the Gospel, with its solemn repetition of phrases and key words and themes, sets it apart from the Synoptic Gospels. On the other hand, the Greek of the Book of Revelation is not so refined. Some have even called it barbaric! In both vocabulary and style, it is so completely different from the Gospel that most commentators agree the two books must have come to us from different hands.

Second, the theology of the two books is very different. Remember, in the Gospel of John we find realized eschatology, the idea that the kingdom of God is already present among us. In the Book of Revelation we find a dualistic or apocalyptic outlook on the end of the world. Would one author hold two such different ideas? It is not likely.

Who, then, is the John of the Book of Revelation? Is it the same person who wrote the Gospel? Probably not. Is it some other person who was also named John? Possibly. Or is it a pseudonym, used to give the book a little more authority than the real author might claim? Possibly. The theories about the authorship of the book abound. We do not need to go into this matter in detail.

For our purposes, what is important is to know that there is some significant discussion about the authorship and sources of the Book of Revelation. No matter who is truly responsible for the words on the page, the words still speak their strong and haunting message. It is that message that we seek to uncover.

III. Outline

Just as there are many theories about the author of Revelation, so too there are many outlines offered by scholars. The different opinions are based upon their ideas of the sources for the book, the intention of the author, and the role of final editors who gave us the book in its present form. Some outlines are very detailed. We will follow a simple, general outline:

Rev 1:1–20	The Superscription
Rev 2:1–3:22	The Letters to the Seven Churches
Rev 4:1–8:1	The Seven Seals
Rev 8:2–11:19	The Seven Trumpets
Rev 12:1–14:20	The Dragon and the Lamb
Rev 15:1–16:21	The Seven Bowls
Rev 17:1–19:10	The Fall of Babylon
Rev 19:11–22:5	The Coming of Christ
Rev 22:6–21	The Conclusion

IV. Why Was the Book of Revelation Written?

Scholars are in general agreement that the book was composed in the middle of the last decade of the Christian era, somewhere between 95 and 100 C.E. Evidence for this is found by analyzing the symbols of the book and discovering certain reference points to events or people of that approximate time. It was not written as a timetable for future events, but as an analysis of their present situation and how to respond to it.

One reason that the Book of Revelation has captivated the world's attention throughout the centuries is the fact that although it was written to address specific problems of the church at the end of the first century C.E., there is a general message for all time as well. The author draws our attention to the fact that persecution will be followed by God's judgment against those evil people who are causing so much turmoil for the church. After the judgment is rendered against them and in favor of the church, the era of salvation will dawn in all its fullness. In one way, the Book of Revelation is world catastrophe described through the imagination of a poet. There are aspects of this message that are difficult to swallow. As mentioned above, this book's message does not repeat the usual expectations of Christian theology. It is filled with violence, a violence wished for by people who are suffering, a violence perpetrated by the hand of God against the enemies of God's people. This is nothing new in the Bible, and yet it is still difficult for us to understand the role that it played. But it is there and our wishful thinking will not take it away. In the Sermon on the Mount Jesus gives this instruction: "In everything do to others as you would have them do to you" (Matt 7:12). Such advice is nowhere to be found in the Book of Revelation. In its place, hopes for vindication abound.

At the time that the Book of Revelation was written Domitian was emperor of Rome. He ruled from 81 to 96 C.E. It was customary at the time to consider the emperor as a divine being. Emperor worship was part of the cult of the realm. Everybody did it. For pagans who had many gods, what was one more? However, for the Christians and the Jews, such worship was an abomination. It was also considered to be an act of treason. This was the reason for the persecutions. If someone refused to honor the emperor, it was a threat to the political order and well-being of the realm. Such nonsense had to be eliminated. Various emperors took this prerogative in varying degrees of seriousness. Domitian was very serious about his rights.

Since the fledgling Christian communities did not have the military power to overthrow Rome, the master of the known world, they turned to God to fight for them. This book invites Christians to wait for God to act. The other books of the New Testament encourage Christians to be actively involved in the work of establishing the reign of God. This book alone invites violence from God and watchful waiting from people.

At the time, Rome was the only power that existed. There were no other superpowers. The plight of the Christians seemed hopeless. With all that in mind, we can read the symbols and words of Revelation and understand their meaning better. It is a plea for justice, *God's* justice.

V. A Key to the Symbols

John and his fellow Christians lived in a world more aware of and more interested in the transcendent dimension of life than people today tend to be. As a result, symbols were a frequent method of communication that helped to express the inexpressible. They brought the ineffable mysteries of life into focus and made them more understandable. We prefer to focus on what is practical. Consequently, we tend to ignore those aspects of life that inspire us to look beyond our senses, beyond what is right in front of us.

Perhaps this is the reason that people today misunderstand the Book of Revelation. People whose spiritual sensitivity is different, developed along other directions, will find it hard to enter the mind-set of a first-century person who was familiar with all the cultural and religious symbols of that time.

This outline might help you to understand the symbols better.

SYMBOL	GENERAL MEANING
4	the world; the universe
6	imperfection; inadequacy
7	perfection; fullness
10, 100, 1,000	wholeness
12	completion; fullness (twelve tribes, twelve apostles)
3 or $3\frac{1}{2}$	a period of calamity or persecution (not to be understood as a specific period of time)
a third	a large portion
Babylon	Rome; Roman imperial state
desert	spiritual purgation
eyes	knowledge; wisdom
many eyes	infinite wisdom
horns	power (like that of a bull)
crown, diadem	kingship, royal power
lamb	Christ
palm leaves	victory; resurrection*
sword	God's spoken word
trumpet	God's voice

*The upright spines of a palm branch leaf resemble the upright spine of a person.

wings	mobility
woman	a people; the church
black	death
green	sickness; death
gold	royalty; wealth
purple	royalty
red	blood
white	purity, victory

This key to the symbols might help us to adopt more of a first-century frame of mind. One more first-century disposition will likewise be helpful: to place ourselves in the shoes of those Christians who first heard Revelation proclaimed in their assemblies. Then we will be in a good position to appreciate it as its author intended.

Questions for Reflection

1. What are some modern religious symbols?
2. Why is it threatening to some persons to learn that "John" might not be the author of Revelation?
3. Is there someplace today where political troubles give cause for secret, underground literature to develop?
4. Why is it important to know about the cultural and historical details of an era in order to appreciate its literature?

Chapter 3

The Superscription
(Rev 1:1–20)

I. Introduction

Most books have a unified theme that weaves throughout the text. When an author wishes to make it easier to identify a certain theme, the author will tell you about it at the beginning of the book. The author of Revelation wrote such an introduction to his text. In these opening verses we are quickly introduced to the themes and terminology that will appear many times throughout this fascinating and puzzling book.

Not every chapter and verse will have a comment in this guide to the Book of Revelation. We will look at the more significant passages. The reader is encouraged to have a good contemporary translation available for consultation.*

"The revelation of Jesus Christ, which God gave him to show his servants what must soon take place; he made it known by sending his angel to his servant John, who

---

*Some recommended Bibles are the New Revised Standard Version (NRSV) or the New American Bible. This study uses the NRSV.

testified to the word of God and to the testimony of Jesus Christ, even to all that he saw. Blessed is the one who reads aloud the words of the prophecy and blessed are those who hear and who keep what is written in it; for the time is near" (Rev 1:1–3).

The name of the book comes from its Greek name, *Apocalypse,* taken from the first few words of the book. An apocalypse is a revelation, an opening up of the future. Only God knows the future. People can only try to control their futures, but in fact it is God who is the Lord of History.

What is to be revealed here? It is nothing less than the future of the world—what God plans to do on behalf of people who are suffering and what God plans to do with those who are causing their suffering. It is a sneak preview of the end of the world and the beginning of the kingdom of God. The style of writing used throughout is apocalyptic, as you read in Chapter 1.

Notice the use of courtroom terminology: witness and testimony. In a sense, the entire book is a court scene. Jesus is the primary witness before God. His testimony is true. There is a pun in the word *witness*, for it not only means "giving testimony to what one has seen or heard or done," but in Greek it is also the word for martyr. Jesus is both the first martyr, the one killed for his obedience to God's way, and also the witness before God.

Witnessing to the Word is often a foreign concept to contemporary Christians. To early Christians, however, it was one of the finest ways to experience the presence of the Risen Lord: to witness to him through his Word—to keep his teaching and spirit alive by remembering it, by talking about it, especially as the sacred books of the New Testament were beginning to be written and accepted. It was a form of spirituality.

Here, the author inserts himself into the mainstream of biblical prophecy, for the prophets of Israel were also visionaries, men who saw God's viewpoint about what needed to happen, and then used words to talk about and interpret that experience. They saw the world through God's eyes. They felt about the world as the Creator felt about it. They wrote about it with human words, in human accents. At a time when persecution—sometimes just local, other times more widespread—was occurring, it took a great deal of courage to be a faithful witness. It was easier and safer to give up.

Notice that the message does not directly come from God. It is mediated through a carefully constructed chain of command: God to Jesus, Jesus to an angel/messenger, the angel to John, and finally John to us. This is typical of the theology of the time. God, who is all holy, must use intermediaries in order to speak to us. Direct access is not possible.

The reward for fidelity to God's Word is "happiness." These words were proclaimed in the solemn liturgical gatherings of the people. These people were familiar with such images from the Bible. The servants of the Lord of the Old Testament are evoked here. A servant is one who hears the word of the master and is obedient to that word. The reward offered for such faithful witness, obedience, is happiness. We find such happiness listed in the Sermon on the Mount, in the Beatitudes (Matt 5:3–12). We also find it in Psalm 1. The sense of the word here is a happiness that comes from experience, from trying a way of life and seeing its wisdom. In the Book of Revelation this formula of happiness occurs seven times. Seven is a favorite number for the author and for the people of that time, a number designating fullness and completeness.

Because of the urgency of the situation in the churches and because of the theological questioning that was taking place and the physical and practical problems that were confronting early Christianity, readers are told that the answers to their questions and the solution to their problems will take place "very soon." This is indeed a message of comfort.

In this "superscription" the author's familiarity with Semitic (Jewish) styles of writing continues to make itself evident. It was a favorite literary device of ancient Jewish authors to begin and end a piece of writing with the same words or general theme. The Book of Revelation will end with a similar blessing regarding the words of the book. Read Revelation 22:6–21 and compare it to Revelation 1:1–3. This technique is called inclusion or Semitic inclusion.

II. The Epistolary Address (Rev 1:4–8)

"John to the seven churches that are in Asia: Grace to you and peace from him who is and who was and who is to come, and from the seven spirits who are before his throne, and from Jesus Christ, the faithful witness, the firstborn of the dead, and the ruler of the kings of the earth…. 'I am the Alpha and the Omega,' says the Lord God, who is and who was and who is to come, the Almighty" (Rev 1:4–8).

From the introduction the author moves to a new form of writing, the form of a letter. The beginning is typical of ancient letters, which all began with a similar greeting. For other examples read the first few verses of any of the Epistles of Paul.

Notice that the greetings are sent to seven of the churches. These seven churches will be representative of the general condition of the church. The seven spirits are probably a reference to the guardian spirits of these churches, a symbol borrowed from Judaism.

These early Christian churches, which are also cities, were not much larger than a typical modern parish community. Each community was its own "church" or assembly for worship. The revelation is addressed primarily to them. Each letter was probably a circular letter, meant to make its way through the community.

The title used for God is based on the revelation of God's sacred name in Exodus 3:14 (I AM WHO I AM). The usual formula referred to God's existence: who was, who is, and who will be. In Revelation this customary formula is adapted to fit the book's theme. It is changed to "who was, who is, and who is to come," accenting a favorite theme, the consolation that God is coming soon to judge the world.

This is a world that is presently ruled by unjust earthly kings. The domination of tyrants is soon to end. By his own faithful obedience to God Jesus is now constituted as the King of all earthly kings. The confrontation between God's idea of kingship and justice and earthly kings and their viewpoint of justice is nothing new in the Bible. For other examples, read the confrontation between Elijah and Ahab in 1 Kings 17–19, or the meeting of Isaiah and Ahaz in Isaiah 7. The same confrontation takes place between Jesus and Pilate when they discuss the meaning of kingship in John 18:33–38.

The Book of Revelation is a "bloody" book. Many people (God's enemies who are also the persecutors of the early Christians) will be eliminated. Blood also represents the salvific action of Jesus on the cross. Early theology about Jesus already emphasized this point, a point made obvious in the liturgical celebration of the Eucharist, "This is my blood, given for you."

III. The First Vision (Rev 1:9ff.)

"I, John, your brother who share with you in Jesus the persecution and the kingdom and the patient endurance, was on the island called Patmos because of the word of God and the testimony of Jesus. I was in the spirit on the Lord's day, and I heard behind me a loud voice like a trumpet saying, 'Write in a book what you see and send it to the seven churches, to Ephesus, to Smyrna, to Pergamum, to Thyatira, to Sardis, to Philadelphia, and to Laodicea'" (Rev 1:9–11).

In these introductory words John addresses the immediate situation of the churches. Although seven specific areas are mentioned, the number 7 would indicate that he is speaking to the universal church as well. These seven are singled out as representative of the successes and failures inherent in the churches at the time.

John awakens one day on the isle of Patmos, a small island measuring about 16 square miles, off the shore of Ephesus (modern Izmir, Turkey). He is there because he gave witness. His message about Christ's kingship was not tolerated by the representatives of the earthly king, the Roman Caesar. For this reason he is sent into exile, probably with the intent of silencing his preaching. The punishment had the opposite effect: it gave him time to produce this amazing document.

There on Patmos, he reflects on what is happening to him and his church. He hears the voice of God call to him as through a trumpet. To compare God's voice to a trumpet is a customary convention in the Bible. For other examples, read Exodus 19:16 and Ezekiel 3:12.

Before the invention of bound books, all writing was done on scrolls. The scrolls were usually made of stretches of parchment, sewn together. They opened horizontally, that is, from right to left, not up and down. (Excellent examples of this ancient technique were discovered at Qumran, where the Dead Sea Scrolls were hidden in nearby caves.) John is told to be a faithful messenger and to write down the visions he will soon experience.

The recipients of these words are the seven specific churches listed. These seven were located on a kind of circular road in Asia Minor. A Roman judge probably traveled from city to city on this road to dispense justice. These small but energetic communities in Asia Minor were often the direct result of the preaching of St. Paul a generation before the Book of Revelation was written. They would flourish there until the Byzantine era, only to disappear with the advent of Islam in the seventh century.

Often the Old Testament prophets describe their religious experiences with an imagery that defies human imagination. After all, how can any of us adequately relate our dreams and visions? Here, John describes his vision of Jesus by combining a number of Old Testament images that would have been familiar to the audience.

The image that strikes us is the familiar one of the Word of God as a two-edged sword. It is a sword of judgment (cf. Isa 49:2; and Heb 4:12). The Word that calls us to decision will also judge us according to our decisions — for or against Jesus and his Word.

IV. Conclusion

In this opening chapter of Revelation we see the themes of judgment and witness that will echo throughout the subsequent chapters. Keep these themes in mind as we continue our journey into John's dreams.

Questions for Reflection

1. Why is it appropriate to think of God's Word as a trumpet? as a sword?

2. What theological picture of Jesus do you discern from this introduction?

3. What do you think? Is the idea of "vision" difficult for modern readers because of our knowledge of psychology?

4. John is in political/theological exile. What modern heroes/heroines suffer because of their positions against the "powers that be"?

5. Compare the image of Christ in Revelation 1:14 to that of Daniel 7:9. What are the parallels? Why would John intentionally do this?

6. Who are the real recipients of the letters?

7. What happened between the time Paul wrote his political advice to Titus (Titus 3:1) and the time John wrote the Apocalypse? Which position is most typical today in your country? in other places?

8. In the United States there are laws governing the relationship between religion and the state. In what ways is this advantageous for both? Are there any unfortunate effects?

Chapter 4

The Letters to the Seven Churches (Rev 2:1–3:22)

I. Introduction

The letters to the seven churches open the first vision of John. Letters were a common means of communication in the ancient world. These letters, like those of St. Paul, were written for public reading. They would form part of the liturgical services of these various communities. Even today the pope and bishops write letters when they wish to communicate an official teaching to the larger church, and these letters are spread about to their audiences.

The letters in Revelation summarize the condition of the church in Asia Minor at the end of the first Christian century. They use highly symbolic language, and they freely borrow images from the secular society of the time and from the Old Testament. We are able to get a good idea of what the church was like at the time in that area of the world. Some people might feel relieved in seeing that, just as today, the community of believers had problems.

If we read all the letters at once, we would notice a recurring pattern in each of them. The author probably did this for effect as well as to make his message somewhat easier to remember.

The Seven Lampstands (Rev 2:2)

The letters follow this general pattern:

1. **"To the presiding spirit of the church in** *(name of city)*, **write"**: Each letter begins with this introduction, specifying the community that is receiving the message.

2. **A "messenger formula"**: The power of the words depended upon the authority of the sender. This same messenger formula is found in the prophetic books the Old Testament. The word that the prophet spoke had authority because it was actually the Word of God. There is a good example of this in the prophet Amos. Read Amos 1:3, 1:6, and 1:9. In Revelation's letters the sender of the message is Jesus. In each letter Jesus will be described in very poetic imagery.

3. **Blessings:** ("I know" formula): For each of the communities the speaker lists a series of qualities that distinguish the local church. These are the accomplishments each group has achieved in faith. They are signals that the people are indeed listening to the Word and living it.

4. **Curses** *("what I have against you")*: After listing the favorable elements of the community, the author lists the areas in which they are failing.

5. **Call to repentance:** One of the most important concepts in the prophets was the call to repentance, that is, to change the lifestyle of a community. It is also one of the first words Jesus speaks in the gospel. (Mark 1:5). This call to repentance, *metanoia*, meant

a rethinking of attitudes and beliefs that would result in a change of behavior.

6. **Promise that the Lord is coming soon:** In the superscription we read for the first time this important theme of the Book of Revelation. There is an urgency about the Christian message. Repentance must take place now. Tomorrow is too late. The Lord is coming soon. Be ready!

7. **Summons to hear:** We also read this in the superscription. The Christian communities are summoned to pay attention to these words of their Lord. Hearing implies obedience and implementation. In Israel's great creed of faith we read these words, "Hear, O Israel: The LORD is our God, the LORD alone" (Deut 6:4). This is an example of the call to obedient listening.

8. **Promises:** The speaker offers rewards to those who pay attention to the words of the letters. The reward is usually the promise of eternal life with Jesus.

This whole pattern is reminiscent of the Old Testament covenant between God and Israel. There are stipulations, there are blessings and curses, rewards and punishments. For further insight, read Exodus 20 and Deuteronomy 28. The analogy would not have been lost on the audience.

The Old Testament theology of the power of the word is presumed here. Once a word is spoken it is real. It has power. It cannot be erased or undone. For example, once Isaac had blessed his trickster son, Jacob, he could not undo his words. He could not revoke the blessing (cf. Gen 27; Isa 55:10–11).

II. Letters

The letters introduce us to all that will follow. Although each individual letter might have been addressed to a specific community, its contents would have been shared with all the others eventually. The letters were circulated to the important cities of western Asia Minor, cities where Christianity was taking hold and struggling to survive both external threats and internal difficulties.

1. Ephesus (Rev 2:1–7). The first letter is written to Ephesus. At the time, near the end of the first century C.E., Ephesus was an important commercial center. It was large enough for the Romans to station a proconsul there, even though neighboring Pergamum was the actual capital. We know that St. Paul preached at Ephesus, staying there over two years. One of his letters was written to that community.

The city's location on the Cayster River helped it to grow into a metropolitan area. It was a crossroads for merchants and travelers going north and south. Population estimates for the time hover around 250,000. Its ruins are among the most extensive and most impressive of Asia

Minor. One of the Seven Wonders of the Ancient World was its Artemision, the temple to Artemis. It also boasted a large gymnasium and one of the largest theaters of the Roman world.

As the river silted up, as it did several times in history, the city was ultimately abandoned. Its splendid ruins became the building stones of pilfering marauders. Before that happened, however, a great Christian church dedicated to Mary was built at Ephesus. Two early ecumenical councils were held there.

In the Book of Revelation, the city is blessed for its patient endurance of hardships and for resisting the teaching of the heretical group known as the Nicolaitans. The seven stars that Christ holds surely represent the brilliance of the city, yet it is Christ who holds/controls that destiny. John concludes his letter with a warning because the people are losing their early enthusiasm for the gospel.

2. Smyrna (Rev 2:8–11). The large modern Turkish city of Izmir is built on the site of ancient Smyrna. Like Ephesus, ancient Smyrna was located on the banks of a river, the Hermus, as it emptied into the Aegean Sea. By all accounts, it was a splendid place. As the letter indicates, Smyrna was known for its wealth and the glory of its buildings. Great temples dotted Mount Pagos. Like Ephesus, Smyrna was a free city with all the rights that entailed for its citizenry. Smyrna was also known for its unquestioned allegiance to Rome.

One of the first great Christian martyrs hailed from Smyrna. His name was Polycarp, and he was the first bishop of the church there. Tradition says that he was a disciple of John the Apostle. Judaism had taken strong hold there. Those first followers of Jesus had a difficult time. Even though the city itself was wealthy, they were very poor. It was often the poor who were attracted to the message of Jesus, a fact that made the first Christians loathsome to native populations.

John commends the believers at Smyrna for their endurance in the midst of all the social and political tribulation they had to face. He writes nothing negative about them.

3. Pergamum (modern Bergama) (Rev 2:12–17). In Revelation 2:12–17, John addresses the inhabitants of this ancient provincial capital of Rome. It was located north of ancient Smyrna, also on a river. The Roman provincial government was located there, making it a pivotal city in Asia Minor. This was a natural development since Pergamum had been a regional capital for almost half a millennium already. Excavations there uncovered a city of splendor: a colonnaded marketplace, a temple to Zeus, a temple to Athena, and a temple to Asklepios, the healing god. Mineral springs helped to develop its reputation as a place of healing. The great Hippocrates worked here. A great parchment library helped to make it a city of knowledge as well.

Although the stories of healings, which are so significant in the Gospels, might have been of interest to the inhabitants, there was a very strong cult in Pergamum to the Roman emperor as a divinity. Without doubt there would be a clash between those who believed in this cult and the early Christians, whose allegiance was to Jesus. Many martyrs would come from Pergamum, and the letter that John addresses to them acknowledges this. As a political prisoner himself on the island of Patmos, he knew too well that reality. They are blessed for holding fast to the name of Jesus despite the cultural pressures against them. John also scolds those who believe in the false prophet and the heretical teachings of the mysterious Nicolaitans.

4. Thyatira (Rev 2:18–29). The fourth of the letters is addressed to Thyatira. Thyatira was known for its purple dye industry, a profitable business because of the demand for royal purple. The town was located in Asia Minor, between Pergamum and Sardis. Like the other cities, it was on a river, the Lycus. The modern town is called Akhisar. Its location, on the main road west to Pergamum, made it a trade and commercial center.

There were many cults at Thyatira, so the cult of Christianity would not have been as noticeable as it was at other locations. Here, however, there probably a social pressure that made life difficult for Christians. Because it was a trade center, the trade guilds held their meetings, often meals, in temples. Christians would not participate in such activities. The author commends the people for their endurance but also scolds them for tolerating the teachings of a certain "Jezebel," a false prophetess whose name would stir up images of the Jezebel of the Old Testament (1 Kgs 16).

5. **Sardis (Rev 3:1–6).** Even in ancient times cities like Sardis had already seen their glory. By the time of the Book of Revelation, its importance, although considerable, was diminished. Hundreds of years before this time, Sardis (modern Sard) had been a great capital. Like the other cities in these letters, it was located on the banks of a river (the Pactolus) and the slopes of a mountain (Mount Tmolus). Once an administrative center, it still had importance as part of the great road that led west to Pergamum. It was part of the Great Postal Road of the ancient Persian empires. Its wealth was legendary.

Its wool industry brought it wealth that made it rather libertine and luxurious. Its reputation gave it a name, but John makes sport of that reputation and refers to a more important name, the name "Christian." Excavations have revealed a synagogue, a gymnasium, a colonnaded street, and many temples.

Given the comfortable nature of life in Sardis, it is easy to imagine parallels to contemporary Christianity. Unlike other areas where the communities were under attack from outside forces, the Christians of Sardis were tranquil. That tranquility, charges the author, led to a softness of faith and a fall from the initial zeal of conversion to Christ.

6. Philadelphia (Rev 3:7–13). The modern name of this "city of brotherly love" is Alasehir. Legend says it truly was a city of brotherly love. It may have been named this by Eumenes II, king of Pergamum, in honor of his brother Attalos. Ancient coins depict the brothers. Like Sardis, it is near the slopes of Mount Tmolus. It would be an understatement to say that this town had a shaky history: it was subject to frequent earthquakes.

On the trade route, it was a wealthy city. Its rulers exacted tax and tribute from passing caravans and travelers. The many shrines and temples provided a steady income for the pagan cults. Christianity was seen as an economic rival. Although the number of Christians was evidently small, the faith of the people was deep. Despite the pressures they surely endured from their pagan neighbors, John commends their stability. He has nothing negative to say about them.

7. Laodicea (Rev 3:14–22). The modern name for this town is Denizli-Gonjali. Its original name was given to it by Antiochus II in honor of his wife and queen, Laodice. Its history is one of constant vanquishment by foreign powers. The great earthquake of 17 C.E., which destroyed many of the cities we have been reading about, dealt a deathblow to Laodicea. It was never restored to its former position. It, too, was built on a river, the Lycus. St. Paul wrote a letter to this community, but it vanished already in ancient times. Its location in the fertile valley made it an important commercial city. Its position likewise had strategic importance on the trade road leading east and west.

Laodicea raised a unique black wool and was famous for medicinal springs. Archaeologists have discovered ruins of theaters, baths, and a gymnasium. A center for healing, it was particularly famous for eye ointments. In Revelation 3:18, John advises the inhabitants to use this famous ointment to clarify their vision of faith. The wealth of the community has made it proud. John has nothing to commend here. In this last letter, we read only of the tepidity of faith and the harsh result: these people will be vomited out of Christ's mouth. Despite their material riches, they are spiritually poor.

III. Conclusion

These communities reflect a cross-section of early church life. In city after city we are able to discern some common difficulties. These were usually struggles between the Jewish synagogues (which were well established in these cities) and the nascent Christian communities. Likewise, there was a struggle between the pagan cults and the churches. These cults had existed for a long time. They were used to having power and influence over people's lives. In many cases they were also supported by the Roman government. The problem was always one of remaining faithful—of giving witness to Jesus—despite overwhelming cultural pressures.

False teachers were also a vexing problem. The New Testament, as we know it, had not yet been written. There was little foundation for those early believers to turn to for help. The Nicene Creed would not come into existence for another 250 years. Christians were struggling to understand their new faith. At the same time there were many interpretations of that faith. Not all of them were accurate. Some of the false interpretations were not necessarily malicious in intent, but they were wrong nonetheless and caused a lot of difficulty. Whom do you listen to?

One special group that is singled out in this regard is the "Nicolaitans." Just who they were or what they taught cannot be determined. We do know this: they surely caused a great deal of controversy in Asia Minor. The general content of their teaching was that it was good to satisfy the lusts of the flesh. It was likewise acceptable to eat the flesh of animals that had been sacrificed to pagan gods. They might have been members of a Gnostic sect, that is, a group of people who claimed to have private revelations about divinities. Only people who had been initiated into their secret knowledge were part of the club.

John certainly knew these cities well. He points to their specific problems with amazing precision. He also demands that each community mend its ways by applying the right remedy for its particular situation. There are no generic cures.

A common thread that runs through each of the difficult situations that these communities faced was mediocrity. Even then it was easy to get comfortable with Christianity. That tepidity of faith was so hateful to John that he writes, "So, because you are lukewarm, and neither cold nor hot, I am about to spit you out of my mouth" (Rev 3:16). It is a problem that is as new as it is old.

Questions for Reflection

1. What is the pattern for conversion (change) that is necessary for the Christian life?
2. List the rich variety of images for life and death contained in the letters.
3. Locate the various cities on a map.
4. Study the episodes alluded to: Jezebel (1 Kgs 21:1–14).
5. In what ways are these ancient problems paralleled in our times?
6. What specific blessings and problems do you find in your parish? in your diocese? in the universal church?
7. Why is tepidity of faith so lethal?

Chapter 5

The Seven Seals
(Rev 4–8:1)

I. Introduction

John's second vision begins here. The sense of urgency continues. It is almost as though he is out of breath, reporting rapidly the spectacular things he is seeing. He is moving us along quickly toward the culmination of history. There is no time to waste.

We get the chance at the beginning of this vision to peek into God's own throne room. The palaces of earthly kings were spectacular, much greater than the homes of ordinary people. It follows that the divine throne room must be many degrees better than any human or royal home. The trumpet-like voice summons John to the open door that leads to heaven and throne room of God. Here is how the author describes the scene:

"After this I looked, and there in heaven a door stood open! And the first voice, which I had heard speaking to me like a trumpet, said, 'Come up here, and I will show you what must take place after this.' At once I was in the spirit, and there in heaven stood a throne, with one seated on the throne! And the one seated there looks like jasper and carnelian, and around the throne is a rainbow that looks like an emerald. Around the throne are twenty-four thrones, and seated on the thrones are twenty-four elders, dressed in white robes, with golden crowns on their

The Twenty-Four Elders (Rev 4:4)

heads. Coming from the throne are flashes of lightning, and rumblings and peals of thunder, and in front of the throne burn seven flaming torches, which are the seven spirits of God; and in front of the throne there is something like a sea of glass, like crystal.

"Around the throne, and on each side of the throne, are four living creatures, full of eyes in front and behind: the first living creature like a lion, the second living creature like an ox, the third living creature with a face like a human face, and the fourth living creature like a flying eagle. And the four living creatures, each of them with six wings, are full of eyes all around and inside. Day and night without ceasing, they sing, 'Holy, holy, holy, the Lord God the Almighty, who was and is and is to come'" (Rev 4:1–8).

How can anyone describe God? The author of Revelation uses many images from the Book of Daniel. That author, too, tried to describe God. He wrote, "As I watched, thrones were set in place, and an Ancient One took his throne, his clothing was white as snow, and the hair of his head like pure wool; his throne was fiery flames, and its wheels were burning fire" (Dan 7:9). Any effort to anthropomorphize God, to depict God in human language or image, is doomed to fail. This image in Daniel is responsible for the stereotypical image of God as an old man. Now it is John's turn to experience the ineffable. There are no words that can adequately express his religious experience, so he turns to descriptive words, to religious poetry. He mixes some well-known images from the Hebrew Bible (Old Testament) with several of his own.

In this passage in Revelation we see images of the Temple of Solomon (2 Chr 3–5), the vision of Ezekiel (Ezek 1:1–28), the dream of Daniel (Dan 7:9–10), and the throne room scene of Isaiah (Isa 6:1–6). A prophet occasionally needs to defend himself and his right to speak in God's name. Now he can say, "I stood in the court of God!" This authority is far more important than that of earthly emperors or kings who had sent John into exile on Patmos.

In this passage there are more elements of apocalyptic. These words and phrases are beginning to become familiar. In these readings priceless gems glisten in the rainbow. There are twenty-four thrones representing the twelve tribes of Israel and the twelve apostles. The number 12 signifies fullness. These elders are clothed in white, the color of victory and purity.

The theophany (appearance of God) is described in typical biblical terms of thunder and lightning. This is the way the image-less God appeared to Moses on Sinai (Exod 19:16–19; Ps 29). It is language that is used to express the transcendence of God. Here God reigns supreme. The divine throne is surrounded by a sea of glass. Not only was glass a very expensive commodity at the time, but the sea is a reminder of the Bronze Sea before the Temple in Jerusalem which was used to signify God's power over watery chaos (Gen 1:1–2; Exod 15).

The four living creatures that surround the throne are borrowed from Ezekiel 1:10. The number 4 is a number of universality, the four cardinal points of the compass. The lion represents nobility, and the bull is a symbol of strength. The man is wisdom personified. The eagle signals swiftness. The wings represent mobility, and the eyes are signs of knowledge. So many eyes signify that there is a great deal of knowledge.

An eternal liturgy takes place in this heavenly throne room. There is chanting and much incense. All of this imitates Temple worship. The angelic choir sings the same song that Isaiah heard—"holy, holy, holy." What appropriate adjectives for the all-holy God! The final epithet is the title for God we saw in Revelation 1:4.

II. The Lamb and the Scroll (Rev 5:1–14)

The scroll contains the next message. The author deliberately toys with his audience. Everyone wants to know what it contains, but first a search must be made to find the one worthy enough to break open the seals and read the secret contents. It is not just sealed once as most documents were. It is sealed seven times. People have been waiting for a long time. The prophet Daniel sealed up a scroll long ago. It contained a message that would not be revealed until the end of time (Dan 12:4). That time has now come.

"You are worthy to take the scroll and to open its seals, for you were slaughtered and by your blood you ransomed for God saints from every tribe and language and people and nation" (Rev 5:9a).

It is Jesus alone who is worthy to break open the seals of testimony. He is worthy because he was faithful to his mission and was slain for his obedience. The heavenly court is a scene of approbation and exuberant rejoicing. Someone who can deliver this great message has been found!

The Lamb is nothing like the gentle image of the Lamb of God in John 1:36. The Greek word here refers to a ram, a powerful leader of the flock. This image of the conquering ram is used in another apocalyptic work written around this same time. That ram, too, conquers those who are making God's people suffer (cf. 1 Enoch 89, 90).

III. The Four Horsemen of the Apocalypse

The first four seals are opened in rapid succession. Imagine the surprise of the reader as horses jump out of the scroll. It is something like an ancient version of a child's "pop-up" book. There are four horsemen, symbolizing the universal destruction to be unleashed upon the earth.

In ancient times the sound of invading armies did not consist of the roaring of mighty machinery like tanks and bombers. Instead, it was the dreaded sound of hundreds of horses' hooves pounding on the earth. The dust cloud they raised would be an advance warning of their approach. The neighing of horses, the clanging of iron weapons, the screams of pain and terror—all these things signaled destruction and the chaos of battle.

The first horseman appears on a white steed, armed with only a bow. The audience understood well the subtle irony of this statement. Of all the earth's armies, only one had embarrassed Rome by refusing to be conquered. These were the Parthians. They came from the east, from the land of the ancient Tigris and Euphrates. In 62 C.E. they dealt a blow to Roman pride. It was not forgotten. To those still suffering from Roman domination, the white horses of the Parthians and their skillful use of the bow were hopeful signs of Rome's demise at some future time.

The next horses will signal blood (red), famine (black), and death (green). They arrive in quick succession. John announces that the Day of the Lord has finally arrived: "for the great day of their wrath has come, and who is able to stand?" (Rev 6:17).

IV. The Sealing of the Thousands (Rev 7:1–17)

After all of this frantic activity it is time for a break. Almost like a television program where a producer shifts from one setting to another, we move from the horrible destruction that is taking place on the earth to the tranquillity and beauty of the heavenly throne room. The liturgy is continuing where it left off in Revelation 5.

As a sign of hope to those experiencing turmoil on the earth, there is a scene that pictures reward for fidelity. Like the Passover in Egypt, where the people of God were saved from the tenth plague, the death of the firstborn, the people of God will once again be marked with a sign of protection (Exod 11:1–12:30).

This marking of the 144,000 is one of the readings for the Holy Day liturgy of All Saints Day. It is a reminder that all of God's people are blessed, holy, and saved. The language is obviously symbolic of the twelve tribes of Israel, since 12,000 from each tribe are saved. All who are faithful are saved. The number 12, a number of completeness, multiplied beyond imagination, is the number saved. It would be a great mistake to limit the capacity of God's kingdom to 144,000, although there are some religions that attempt to do that.

Note the tender ending of this section: "for the Lamb at the center of the throne will be their shepherd, and he will guide them to springs of the water of life, and God will wipe away every tear from their eyes" (Rev 7:17).

If anyone has the image of Revelation as a book of destruction and violence, they need to read these passages too. The Lamb, which normally is led by a shepherd, becomes the shepherd. "I am the good shepherd" (John 10:14; Ps 23). In lands where water is often scarce, the Lamb will lead them, not just to brackish cisterns, but to springs of fresh water (Jer 2:13; John 4:10, 14).

V. Conclusion

We are at the end of the section on the seven seals. We might expect that all this activity would end with the opening of the seventh seal, the climactic number. But the action will continue. It is time for another time out.

"When the Lamb opened the seventh seal, there was silence in heaven for about half an hour. And I saw the seven angels who stand before God, and seven trumpets were given to them" (Rev 8:1–2).

Within one paragraph, the number 7 appears three times. The symbolism speaks for itself. Just as everyone is ready to see the end, there is a pause. All of heaven literally holds its breath, waiting to see the results of the opening of the seventh seal. The silence is deep, eerie. One can sense the air of expectation. What is next?

Questions for Reflection

1. Why does the author use so many themes and images from other biblical sources?
2. Why would some religions try to limit the number of the "saved" to only 144,000?

3. The heavenly courtroom is filled with praise for God. Just what is praise, and why is it a proper form of prayer?

4. The heavenly worship consists of the refrain of "amen." What does this term mean, and why should we be careful about its use?

5. What is your response to the almost violent shifting of scenes from earthly destruction to heavenly beauty? Why would the author do this?

6. What modern scourges might the horsemen bring?

Chapter 6

The Seven Trumpets
(Rev 8:2–11:19)

I. Introduction

At the end of the previous section we were left in expectation of future events. A great silence descended in the heavenly throne room. As the silence deepened, so did the wonder at what would happen next. Seven trumpet blasts will shatter the stillness. Each blast will also shatter the complacency of the earth. The trumpets spew out notes that are dissonant and plague-filled. Such is the revelation of the trumpets.

We are still peeking into John's vision. He is still peeking into the heavenly throne room. There, in the midst of the cosmic liturgy, the vision of Isaiah 6 continues. The heavenly liturgy is a perfect form of our earthly liturgy. There is incense, an altar, people, and prayers. The acolyte in heaven, however, does not handle the censer with grace. The burning coals are hurled down to earth. The heavens thunder and a brilliant display of lightning flashes through the sky (cf. Ps 29). The earth trembles in anticipation and fear at what is about to take place.

II. The First Four Trumpets (Rev 8:6–13)

The disasters affecting the earth should be taking a terrible toll on the ecology and human life. But the earth

The Seven Trumpets (Rev 8–11)

is stubborn. Hard-heartedness, like that of Pharaoh in Egypt, seems stronger than God's power—or even stronger than common sense. The first four trumpets, like the first four seals, appear in quick succession and pour out their contents upon the earth. Trumpets are used to warn people about impending disaster. Their shrill notes cause heads to perk up and eyes to search for an approaching enemy (Jer 4:5). On a more positive note, on the Day of the Lord the trumpet will sound and gather the exiles back home (Isa 27:13). That's the good news.

The trumpets contain a strange medley of biblical prophecy, Exodus imagery, and the creative touch of the author.

	TRUMPET	EXODUS	PROPHET
1.	hail, fire, blood (Rev 8:7)	Exod 9:24 (hail)	- - - (Ps 18:13)
2.	flaming mountain fish and ships destroyed (Rev. 8:8–9)	Exod 7:18 (fish die in the polluted Nile)	Jer 51:25
3.	falling star polluted water (wormwood) (Rev 8:10–11)	- - - -	Isa 14:12 (song against the king of Babylon)
4.	darkness (Rev 8:12)	Exod 10:21–29	Amos 8:9; Joel 2:3 (Day of the Lord)

These disasters fall upon the earth, yet the inhabitants do not repent of their evil ways. Each of the trumpets blasts forth a loud reminder of God's past actions — actions against enemies, but on behalf of the chosen people. The first section of the trumpet sonata ends with the eerie cry of an eagle, "Woe, woe, woe" (Rev 8:13). *Woe* is a favorite word of the prophets, used to prepare people for the disaster about to come. Here the sound comes from an eagle, whose own call sounds like the word *woe* in Hebrew *(hoy)* (cf. Isa 24:16).

III. The Fifth and Sixth Trumpets (Rev 9:1–21)

The contents of the next two trumpets, like the contents of the fifth and sixth seals, are long, sustained notes. They continue to repeat some of the prophetic and Exodus themes, but they are composed with a new kind of music. It is a kind of free-form jazz. It is mythology. The old images don't adequately express the message anymore, so the author invents new images to make his message stronger and clearer. Great and terrible disaster is approaching, so get ready.

Out of the depths of the abyss the fifth trumpet summons terrible locusts to the surface of the earth (Rev 9:1–11). Even today in farm areas plagues of locust are feared. They devour the crops. Human hunger is their legacy. Notice though, that the locusts here are commanded not to eat crops, but to sting people. So painful is the sting that those afflicted will wish to die but will not be able to.

The physical description of the locusts is fearsome. They are far worse than the little creatures that plagued Egypt (Exod 10:13–15). These bugs are the size of horses! Their long hair resembles that of invading barbarians. (The word *barbarian* means "long hair.")

The sixth trumpet blast (Rev 9:12–21) brings more chaos. A multicolored array of angelic warriors is released from the traditional place of invasion, the East. The unbelievers are devoured by them but not the faithful followers of the Lamb. The invaders come from the territory of the Parthians (first horseman of the Apocalypse, Rev 6:2). Despite their terrible ravaging of the earth, destroying a whole third of humankind, there is no repentance. The hard-heartedness of the unbelievers remains.

IV. The Interlude (Rev 10:1–11:14)

The horrors that the trumpets announce are set loose upon the earth. So intense is the activity and so awful is the result that once again there is need for an intermission. The scene shifts back to heaven. The awesome elements of the theophany continue. Thunder rolls. Rainbows wrap around the sky. The sounds of roaring lions add to the tumult. Clouds envelop the world. God is present.

The lions' voices and thunder recall the voices of the prophets Amos and Joel (Amos 1:2; Joel 3:16). The cloud and rainbow hearken back to the Exodus and Ezekiel (Exod 13:21; Ezek 1:28). A magnificent angel, who always represents a mediator between God and humankind, appears.

The angel gives John another scroll. This one is a small one. John is commanded to eat it, that is, to completely digest its message and to make it his own.

"So I went to the angel and told him to give me the little scroll; and he said to me, 'Take it, and eat; it will be bitter to your stomach, but sweet as honey in your mouth.' So I took the little scroll from the hand of the angel and ate it; it was sweet as honey in my mouth, but when I had eaten it, my stomach was made bitter" (Rev 10:9–10).

The image is meant to remind us of the prophet Ezekiel, who was likewise commanded to eat a scroll with God's word on it (Ezek 2:8–3:3). The scroll is both sweet and sour. It will prophesy sweet victory for God's faithful ones, but not without a price — the sourness of still more suffering to come. John is commissioned again to go forth and speak about his visions.

The next part of the interlude mixes many biblical images and historical events. Jewish law required two witnesses for a trial. The whole Book of Revelation has been a trial. In it God is judging the world. Who are these two witnesses? Perhaps they are Moses and Elijah, who also appeared with Jesus at the Transfiguration (Mark

9:2–13). Popular Jewish legend held that before the end of the world, Elijah would reappear. When questioning his disciples about his identity, some mentioned that perhaps Jesus was the eschatological Elijah (Matt 16:13–20). The plagues that are shaking the earth are all parallel to the great signs that Moses offered Pharaoh (Exod 7:14–11:10). The lampstand and olive trees were mentioned in Zechariah (4:3), one of the last prophets.

Only the terrible mythical beast, rising out of the depths of the pit, can kill these witnesses. The same beast is found in Daniel 7:3–7. This beast, the personification of Roman political and military might, will reappear in Revelation 13 and 17.

Jerusalem is likened to the destroyed city of Sodom and the hated land of Egypt (Ezek 16:26, 48). It was a terrible psychological and theological abomination not to bury corpses. For that reason dying on the battlefield and being left behind for carrion-eating birds was a favorite taunt of ancient armies against one another. Dead bodies were not allowed to remain in the city. It would render it both unsafe and impure. So hated were these two truthful witnesses, prophets who spoke for God, that the evil people of Jerusalem rejoiced at their demise and danced around their unburied bodies. Seldom did Israel's prophets live to an old age. No one wants to be reminded of his or her sinfulness. Here, the entire populace of the evil earth participates in the macabre death dance. John's audience must have often felt the same way—that the entire population around them would dance on their graves.

Yet God will always vindicate the holy ones. God's power over death will be demonstrated again. First, God vindicated his Son, Jesus. In order to express the new life that will eventually rise from the old, the Book of Revelation borrows the imagery of the dry bones prophecy found in Ezekiel 37. These two witnesses will receive their reward and will be carried to heaven. Some of the bystanders will even convert, so powerful is the vision. But their conversion is for the wrong reasons. It will do them no good.

V. The Seventh Trumpet (Rev 11:15–19)

Few sights were as spectacular in the ancient world as the accession to the throne by a new king. It meant spectacle and celebration. The psalms of Israel reflect these glorious occasions.

> "The LORD is king! Let the earth rejoice;
> let the many coastlands be glad!
> Clouds and thick darkness are all around him;
> righteousness and justice are the foundation of his throne.
> Fire goes before him,
> and consumes his adversaries on every side.
> His lightnings light up the world;
> The earth sees and trembles."
>
> (Ps 97:1–4)

This is a psalm that proclaims the kingship of God. Notice how the images of thunder, lightning, and so on are also found throughout the Book of Revelation. In this scene the seventh trumpet is sounded and we witness the coronation of the Anointed One, the Messiah. The reference is to Jesus. (*Messiah*, which means "anointed" in Hebrew, refers to the way the kings were officially established as rulers. The high priest poured oil over the new king's head. All kings were "messiahs." The Hebrew word *messiah* is rendered as *Christos* in Greek. That is how the title "Christ" or "the Christ" gets applied to Jesus who is *the* Messiah.)

The power, which the Anointed One has, is power to once and for all subjugate all earthly kings to the divine power of God. It is a moment of triumph. John (and we along with him) gets a sneak preview of what will occur at the end of the world. Just as God ruled over all the nations (Ps 99:1), now the messianic king will establish the eternal kingdom of God's sovereignty. It is a scene of triumph and celebration. The messianic king has fulfilled the vision of Daniel:

> "As I watched in the night visions,
> I saw one like a human being coming with the
> clouds of heaven.
> And he came to the Ancient One and was
> presented before him.

To him was given dominion and glory and kingship,
that all peoples, nations, and languages should serve him.
His dominion is an everlasting dominion that
shall not pass away,
and his kingship is one that shall never be destroyed."
(Dan 7:13–14)

VI. Conclusion

The nations raged against the kingdom of God (Ps 99:1; Rev 11:18). They have always raged against the truth that their power is really quite limited and their threats really quite empty. God's truth endures forever — and *only* that truth endures forever.

The images of our theological kaleidoscope have once again taken us for a roller coaster ride from the beauty and joy of the heavenly court to the devastation that is loosed upon the earth. Themes sneak into a few verses and then disappear just as suddenly, lurking around the corner to reappear and startle us in some new way.

The book is half completed now, yet the world has not ended. The kingdom has not yet been fully inaugurated. Despite all the variety of action that we have witnessed, John is about to tell us that we haven't seen anything yet!

Questions for Reflection

1. Why do the kingdoms of this world struggle to dominate souls as well as our physical existence?

2. What do you think of John's use of images? Is it creative, boring, frightening?

3. Notice that in order to understand this book of the Bible it is necessary to know the Hebrew Bible (Old Testament) and also to be familiar with history. What can you do to establish a study program in your parish or neighborhood?

4. Does history repeat itself (for example, the way the plagues of Egypt are recapitulated in the Book of Revelation)?

5. This is the halfway point in our reading of Revelation. Which do you sense is stronger—hope or fear? Why?

Chapter 7

The Dragon and the Lamb
(Rev 12:1–14:20)

I. Introduction

From the splendor of the theophany we are taken suddenly to a violent battle in the heavens. We have seen that the whole Book of Revelation is a kind of courtroom drama. Jesus speaks as a witness against the powers of evil. He also speaks on behalf of his white-robed holy ones in heaven and also for those who are faithful on earth. The power of God is pitted against the power of the Roman Empire. Good versus evil. God's Word versus the word of this world. This kind of dualism is found throughout the Book of Revelation.

This is the heart of the apocalyptic vision of John. The destruction and chaos are now so great that the action reaches cosmic proportions. John can only express his vision by means of the most bizarre mythological images. One era of history is ending, the era in which evil held sway. Now the announcement of Jesus, "The kingdom of God has come near" (Mark 1:15), will be fulfilled. It is now the era of the kingdom. It is the time of salvation for all God's people, for those who have held out faithfully in the face of great obstacles.

II. The Dragon and the Lamb (Rev 12:1–6)

"A great portent appeared in heaven: a woman clothed with the sun, with the moon under her feet, and on her head a crown of twelve stars. She was pregnant and was crying out in birthpangs, in the agony of giving birth. Then another portent appeared in heaven: a great red dragon, with seven heads and ten horns, and seven diadems on his heads. His tail swept down a third of the stars of heaven and threw them to the earth. Then the dragon stood before the woman who was about to bear a child, so that he might devour her child as soon as it was born. And she gave birth to a son, a male child, who is to rule all the nations with a rod of iron. But her child was snatched away and taken to God and to his throne; and the woman fled into the wilderness, where she has a place prepared by God, so that there she can be nourished for one thousand two hundred sixty days" (Rev 12:1–6).

Who is this woman? For a long time she was interpreted as Mary, mother of Jesus. It was relatively easy to come to that conclusion, especially by interpreting this passage in the light of Isaiah 7:14, where the woman with child was to give birth to the Messiah. Christian art throughout the centuries has used these verses to depict Mary.

However, the woman is not Mary. John, true to his apocalyptic leanings, mixes many images when he develops his characters. The ancient audience would have known that there was a legend that the sun god, Apollo in

The Woman Clothed in the Sun (Rev 12:1–16)

the Roman pantheon, had a wife. She was called the queen of heaven. There are similar mythic elements in other "woman and dragon" stories in ancient literature. In each of them the dragon threatens the life of an unborn child. The woman in these verses, a combination of many such stories, represents those who must struggle against the power of evil.

The particular religious accents in Revelation come from the Old Testament. Psalm 104, most likely originally a hymn to the Egyptian sun god Aton, speaks about God as one clothed with the sun in splendor. The twelve stars in the woman's crown could represent the twelve tribes of Israel or the twelve apostles. The loud wail of birthpangs evokes the image of Daughter Sion (Zion) calling out (Mic 4:10).

Who is this child? The child represents the eschatological era, ushered into existence by the Messiah. He is taken up into heaven (the ascension) while the woman (those struggling on earth) is left behind to face yet another delay before the fulfillment of the kingdom.

Who is this monster? The Bible, basing its words upon the science of the day, was sure that great monsters lived in the sea. This was a common belief until Columbus proved otherwise. Psalm 74:13 speaks about the dragons in the waters. It makes special reference to Leviathan. In Daniel, we saw the fearsome monsters that represented the political powers of his time. Once again, John uses mythological creatures to express the inexpressible—dragons, the stuff of nightmares. John also offers the comfort that God would ultimately have control over the sea and its monster elements (cf. Ps 89:10).

Why flee to the desert? The desert always had special meaning for Israel. A ten-minute walk south of Jerusalem and one is already in the wasteland. It was a favorite place to be alone. The Gospels tell us that Jesus went there (Matt 4:1–11). It was not without its dangers, however. In the desert, wild animals foraged. Bandits and gypsies encamped there. The Hebrews called it *midbar*, the place of noises. There, in the desert, things went "bump" in the night!

When the Hebrew people left Egypt and wandered in the desert, they should have perished. There was no food or water. Yet, in the desert that represented death, the Hebrew people found life. They found God. There was water and manna. It was in the desert where they came to know God. Consequently, the desert came to represent a place where one could be especially close to God. "Remember the long way that the LORD your God has led you these forty years in the wilderness, in order to humble you, testing you to know what was in your heart, whether or not you would keep his commandments" (Deut 8:2). Another image of the desert ideal is found in the prophet Hosea. "Therefore, I will now allure her, and bring her into the wilderness, and speak tenderly to her"

(Hos 2:16). The desert is a place where God protects his chosen people. Because Israel depended totally upon God alone in the desert, the desert ideal represented the perfect relationship between God and the people.

III. Michael's Victory over the Dragon (Rev 12:7–12)

Michael, the guardian of Israel, fights the battle for God against the dragon. The battle in heaven is a reflection of the struggle on earth between God's people and the imperial Roman power. Good will win, of course. In all of these mythological stories, no matter how powerful the forces of evil, good always conquers evil.

The actual conqueror of Satan has been Jesus. He accomplished this through his ministry. The Gospels clearly depict his works of good (healing the sick, curing the possessed, raising the dead) as breaking the hold that Satan had upon the earth.

But evil is strong. Like a suspense film, just when we feel that we can breathe a sigh of relief, there is a surprise revival of energy in the villain. Here the power of evil, the power of Satan, promises to return in even worse ways than before: "But woe to the earth and the sea, for the devil has come down to you with great wrath, because he knows that his time is short!" (Rev 12:12).

IV. The Dragon Confers Power on the Sea Beast (Rev 13:1–10)

"Then the dragon took his stand on the sand of the seashore. And I saw a beast rising out of the sea, having ten horns and seven heads; and on its horns were ten diadems, and on its heads were blasphemous names. And the beast that I saw was like a leopard, its feet were like a bear's, and its mouth was like a lion's mouth. And the dragon gave it his power and his throne and great authority. One of its heads seemed to have received a deathblow, but its mortal wound had been healed. In amazement the whole earth followed the beast" (Rev 12:18–13:3).

The beast from the sea becomes the dragon's agent on earth. The beast is the negative side of the Lamb, its opposite. The Lamb, the power of goodness, fights on the side of good. The beast, the power of evil, fights against good in order to survive. This beast looks suspiciously like that final beast of Daniel's vision (Dan 7). Of course, it arises out of that dreadful place, the sea.

At the time that the Book of Daniel was written, the final beast represented Antiochus IV Epiphanes. Now the beast represents Rome in general, and Nero in particular, whose anti-Christian reputation is legendary. He had come to the throne through the machinations of his mother, the wife of Claudius, whom she poisoned. There was a popular story about Nero told in those days. He had been severely wounded, but survived. He had been killed, but now was returning. Evil dies hard.

Nero, whose fiddling around Rome is notorious, took his divine prerogatives most seriously. The seven heads on the beast probably are an intentional mockery of the seven hills upon which imperial Rome was built. Nero demanded that people worship him. This was no problem for the pagan Romans, but it was heresy to both Jews and Christians who worshiped the One God. Was Nero dead or alive? Was he coming again to reestablish his authority? In a place where any talk against the emperor was treason, John and his followers did well to speak in highly symbolic language that only they would understand. (I think that John is having a lot of linguistic fun here.)

But it is serious also. The people of the world are always swayed by the apparent authority and attractiveness of the way of the beast, the way of the world. Rome was the only national power that existed at the time. There was no other superpower. There was only Rome. Any hope of conquering this military giant seemed foolish and hopeless. Thus, only God could do it. There will always be those who worship the beast or all the things that the beast represents. Such powers will stop at nothing to keep their way of life safe from criticism or harm. This was part of the persecution that the communities of Asia Minor were experiencing. The section ends with the solemn and unhappy truth that some will die before the final battle takes place: "Let anyone who has an ear listen: If you are to be taken captive, into captivity you go; if you kill with the sword, with the sword you must be killed. Here is a call for the endurance and faith of the saints" (Rev 13:9–10).

V. The Second Beast (Rev 13:11–18)

"Then I saw another beast that rose out of the earth; it had two horns like a lamb and it spoke like a dragon. It exercises all the authority of the first beast on its behalf, and it makes the earth and its inhabitants worship the first beast, whose mortal wound had been healed. It performs great signs, even making fire come down from heaven to earth in the sight of all; and by the signs that it is allowed to perform on behalf of the beast, it deceives the inhabitants of earth, telling them to make an image for the beast that had been wounded by the second and yet lived; and it was allowed to give breath to the images of the beast so that the image of the beast could even speak and cause those who would not worship the image of the beast to be killed. Also it causes all, both small and great, both rich and poor, both free and slave, to be marked on the right hand or the forehead, so that no one can buy or sell who does not have the mark, that is, the name of the beast or the number of its name" (Rev 13:11–17).

The second beast plays a role similar to that of the first beast. This second monster arises out of the earth. Both earth and sea, the opponents of heaven, give rise to evil. There is no escape while still on this side of the kingdom.

Perhaps the first beast represents imperial Rome while the second beast is the power of the local imperial cities. At any rate, its policies are the same as those of the water beast. The function of the second beast is to promote the policies of the first beast. This is not an unwise thing to do if one wishes to court imperial favor — perhaps lessening of local taxes or the investment in some new commercial enterprise in one's colonial setting.

Some commentators think that the sign on the forehead or right hand was a sort of legal paper that gave one the right to participate in the economic life of a city, a kind of identification card that would be denied to people who refused to worship the emperor. Others consider it as a flipside of the mark of baptism, which distinguished Christians from pagans. Still others say that the "mark" is a symbol for the Christian refusal to use the minted coins of the realm, which usually had an image of the emperor, depicted as a divinity.

A famous quotation from this pericope concerns the number of the beast, the infamous 666 of the Book of Revelation: "This calls for wisdom: let anyone with understanding calculate the number of the beast, for it is the

number of a person. Its number is six hundred sixty-six"
(Rev 13:18).

Hebrew does not use Arabic numerals. Numbers were,
and still are, represented by letters of the alphabet—for
instance, A = 1, B = 2, and so on. In Jewish mystical
thought, many fascinating conclusions can be drawn by
playing with this alphabetic-numerical system. For instance,
when taking a collection, people are encouraged to put
eighteen coins in the box. Why? Eighteen is the number of
the "life," the Hebrew word *hay* (pronounced "high").

Using this system, if we write the name "Nero
Caesar" and then add up its equivalent number value, the
total is 666. It is the number of the beast, which is also the
number of a very human man. Nero is the emperor who
is synonymous with the persecution of Christians. This
symbolic use of numbers in Jewish mysticism is called
gematria.

VI. The Proclamation of Imminent Judgment (Rev 14:6–20)

The announcement of judgment has taken place (Rev
14:6–13). Good people will be rewarded. Some are already
singing a glorious song to the Lord in the kingdom, a new
song of astonishing beauty and power (Rev 14:1–5).

The evil kingdom, Rome, is referred to from now on
by another code name—Babylon, that most evil of all

cities in biblical history. The Son of Man, now clearly identified as Jesus, makes his triumphant appearance (Dan 7:13). The earth is ready for harvest (Joel 3:13–16). It is too late for those who still worship the beast.

John recalls all the parables of destruction and judgment. The harvesters are ready for their work (Mark 4:29; Matt 13:39). Harvest always implies judgment and separation, like the separation of sheep and goats.

The harvest has been prepared for a long time. An angel threw the coals down to earth (Rev 8:3–4). An angel revealed the contents of the sixth trumpet (Rev 9:13, with the command to kill a third of humanity). Now an angel begins trampling the grapes of wrath. The image was a familiar harvest image to a biblical audience.

A question is asked of God. "Why are your robes red, and your garments like theirs who tread the wine press?" (Isa 63:2). The answer comes and God speaks: "I have trodden the winepress alone, and from the peoples no one was with me; I trod them in my anger and trampled them in my wrath, their juice spattered on my garments and stained all my robes. For the day of vengeance was in my heart, and the year for my redeeming work had come" (Isa 63:3–4).

For 200 miles around, as high as a horse's bridle, the blood of God's enemies flowed out from the winepress (Rev 14:20). It is an image of awesome destruction, of God's final authority over the earth that God created. Had these people been faithful, they would have been spared. Instead of producing sweet grapes, they produced evil. In Isaiah 27:1–8, the images of the sea beast and unfruitful harvest are also combined. The parable of Israel as a vineyard is a familiar one in the Bible. Read Isaiah 5 to see the full comparison. Here the whole world is the vineyard. It has been crushed.

VII. Conclusion

The action is beginning to move very rapidly. Finally, there is visible vindication for the people of God to see. God is coming to the rescue. Enemies are being destroyed. Blood, the life force, is filling the earth. This is the only reward that comes to those who follow the beast.

The "Battle Hymn of the Republic" has immortalized these images of harvest in song. The stately beauty of the hymn, however, is a grim contrast to the severity of the theological statement. Our notions of a destroying, perennially angry God, come from scenes like this in Revelation. Does the historical and theological context of this book shed a different light on that image?

Questions for Reflection

1. Why are mythological expressions of our human fears and hopes so important? so commonplace in ancient cultures? Do we need new images today?

2. Why does the "power of the world" still seem to hold so much sway? in military spending? in economic power?

3. In what ways does our culture still give homage to the beast? to false security?

4. Why are harvest images appropriate?

5. What new images might be better fit today's culture?

Chapter 8

The Seven Bowls
(Rev 15:1–16:21)

I. Introduction

The final series of seven is about to begin. Each of them has developed in a similar pattern. The first few disasters from the trumpets, seals, and so on pass rapidly before our eyes. The final set of disasters is long and drawn out. Like the previous disasters, almost all of the imagery is borrowed from the plagues in Egypt. This episode of the seven bowls will be no exception. This time, however, the whole earth, not just a part of it, will be afflicted.

The bowls that are emptied upon the earth are the great bronze bowls that were used by the Temple priests. After the sacrifices they would carry the remnants of the ashes from the sacrificial animals away from the altar of holocaust ("You shall make pots for it to receive its ashes, and shovels and basins and forks and firepans; you shall make all its utensils of bronze" [Exod 27:3]). This time the bowls are filled with plagues. The irony would not be lost upon a people whose ancestral Temple had been

85

destroyed by the Romans. When the plagues of the Book of Exodus were taking place (Exod 7:8–11:10), the first nine affected everyone. Only the tenth plague, the death of the firstborn, passed over the Hebrew people. The Hebrews were spared. The Egyptians were not. This time care will be taken to protect all of God's people from all of the plagues in the bowls. The people of God have already been marked for salvation. Only evil people, those who refuse to repent, will perish. When a similar destruction was prophesied by Ezekiel, the people of God were also protected by a saving sign (Ezek 9–10). God takes care of those who believe.

The smoke that filled the air is a sign of divine presence. Here, the presence is angry and judgmental. Smoke was always in the air from the holocaust offerings at the Temple. The concept behind this was that the pleasing odor of the roasting sacrificial meat rose to God, taking with it the sacrifice from the altar. Incense was used to enrich this symbol. Most likely it also had the effect of providing a sweet smell to cover up some of the less savory odors associated with the burning of the sacrifices.

II. The First Five Bowls (Rev 16:1–11)

The plagues poured out from the bowls are familiar ones: festering boils, the sea turning to blood, the rivers and springs (sources of life-giving water) turning to blood, fire, and darkness (Exod 7:14–10:29). These fear-some disasters accomplish only one thing: the followers of the beast entrench. They do not repent. Their stupidity is exceeded only by their stubbornness. The Bible consistently calls such an attitude "hardness of heart."

As the angelic agents pour out the plagues, they sing psalms to God, praising God's justice and judgment. Their lyrics resonate harshly in our ears: "You are just, O Holy One, who are and were, for you have judged these things; because they shed the blood of saints and prophets, you have given them blood to drink. It is what they deserve!" (Rev 16:5–6). The punishment fits the crime. It is perfect retribution.

Such violence grates against our Christian ears. It is important to place these ideas against the situation in which they are taking place, especially the troubled times of these early Christians, and to remember that this is poetic imagery. It is wishful thinking. It is apocalyptic. Nonetheless, such revenge is no stranger to the Bible. For another good example, read Psalm 109. Immediate retribution against enemies was the desire of a people whose notions of an afterlife were vague. Recall, too, that this evil falls upon the enemies of God and the enemies of the people, not upon all (Ps 105). Those who shed the blood of God's righteous people would never go unpunished (cf. Pss 119:137; 145:17).

III. The Sixth Bowl (Rev 16:12–16)

For these last two bowls, like the last trumpets and last seals, the imagery moves away from the familiar territory of the plagues in Egypt and continues to develop the unique mythological elements of the Book of Revelation. So fearsome is the message that only the bizarre nature of myth can express it.

"The sixth angel poured his bowl on the great river Euphrates, and its water was dried up in order to prepare the way for the kings from the east. And I saw three foul spirits like frogs coming from the mouth of the dragon, from the mouth of the beast, and from the mouth of the false prophet. These are demonic spirits, performing signs, who go abroad to the kings of the whole world, to assemble them for battle on the great day of God the Almighty. ('See, I am coming like a thief! Blessed is the one who stays awake and is clothed, not going about naked and exposed to shame.') And they assembled them at the place that in Hebrew is called Harmagedon" (Rev 16:12–16).

The Euphrates River was the home ground of the Parthians, that dreaded white-horsed, armed-with-bows enemy of Rome. God had dried up the water before the Hebrews in order to save them from Pharaoh (Exod 14). God also dried up the Jordan so that his people could cross into the Promised Land (Josh 3:13–17). Now the Euphrates will dry up. All the armies of the world will cross its banks in order to do battle against God's enemies. The natural boundary that prevented them from easily moving into battle is now removed. Earth, beware! (Keep in mind, the earth is still drenched with blood from the trampling of the grapes of wrath [Rev 14:20].)

Ancient warfare was not an impersonal matter of launching rockets, dropping bombs, or shooting guns from a distance. It was hand-to-hand combat. Bows and arrows. Battering rams. Horses. Terrible pain. Blood. This assembly is exactly the opposite of the gathering of the saved in heaven (Rev 14). These hard-of-heart leaders will still fight for absolute possession of the earth. So it always goes with kings and with this world. Like frogs hopping around, the armies come forth. The Bible is filled with the signs of its times. Isaiah had a vision that there would be no more war (Isa 2:4). Zechariah saw the opposite. He saw the ultimate war waged against Jerusalem.

"See, a day is coming for the LORD, when the plunder taken from you will be divided in your midst. For I will gather all the nations against Jerusalem to battle, and the city shall be taken and the houses looted and the women raped; half the city shall go into exile, but the rest of the people shall not be cut off from the city. Then the LORD will go forth and fight against those nations as when he fights on a day of battle. On that day his feet shall stand on the Mount of Olives, which lies before Jerusalem on the east; and the Mount of Olives shall be split in two from east to west by a very wide valley; so that one half of the Mount shall withdraw northward, and the other half southward" (Zech 14:1–4).

The location of the battle in the Book of Revelation is not Jerusalem, where one might expect it to take place. Rather, it is located at Armageddon. Armageddon is a Greek form of the Hebrew word *Har-Megiddo*, that is, the mountain of Megiddo. Megiddo stood in the Plain of Jezreel. There it protected the surrounding countryside. The Great Sea Road, that ancient highway for trade caravans, passed it. Whoever wanted military and economic control of the world had to possess Megiddo.

Modern archeologists have uncovered over twenty cities built one on top of another at this site. Many battles were waged there over the centuries. It was a place of warfare and destruction. Many times its streets ran with the blood of the vanquished. For the author of Revelation, this site, which represented economic and political power, this site that had seen so many battles already, was the natural location for staging the final battle whose purpose was to protect the interests dear to earthly kings, economy and power.

IV. Conclusion: The Seventh Bowl (Rev 16:17–20)

Despite the scene of thunder, lightning, and all the other elements of a theophany, the complete and final end is not yet upon the world. There will be another delay. As always, the purpose of the delay is to build up the suspense level. This time it serves to focus all of our attention on evil Babylon, the symbol for Rome. Special devastation awaits her.

The hard-of-heart still lurk around the earth. Even the inanimate islands and mountains are clever enough to get out of God's way. Hailstones, like those of Egypt, rain upon the earth (Exod 9:23).

The author loves to set us up for the grand finale. He has done so several times already. All that remains on the earth is evil Babylon. Our entire attention is now focused upon this place and its fate.

Questions for Reflection

1. Is the repetition of plagues boring or exciting for modern audiences? Why or why not?

2. Why is warfare always the image of destruction? What other ways do we destroy one another?

3. Locate Armageddon (Megiddo) on a map. Situate it strategically. Read about its role in the Bible: Judg 5:19ff.; 2 Kgs 9:27; 2 Chr 35:20–24.

4. How have modern filmmakers played with the images of the Book of Revelation? Is it fair? Why do films, with their wrong theological interpretations, become more meaningful than the original biblical texts?

Chapter 9

The Fall of Babylon (Rev 17:1–19:10)

I. Introduction

Everyone is waiting for the fall of the evil empire, Babylon. With great skill, the author has pushed us toward this moment. He leads us to the climax and then waits. He stalls. He moves us again. He delays still further. Finally, God's vindication will be directed against Babylon, which is actually representing Rome.

Historically, Babylon fell in 539 B.C.E. to the Persians. That once lofty empire quickly fell apart when confronted by a superior power. When Babylon was in its glorious age, it was splendid. Great temples marked the city skyline. Broad roads and canals (the streams of Babylon, Ps 137) crisscrossed it. As usual in apocalypses, Revelation uses an example of God's past power to proclaim God's intention for the future.

Despite Babylon's greatness, it was the most hated of cities in the Bible. It came to represent all that was against God and the chosen people. The personification of wisdom or foolishness and the personification of cities to represent various human attributes were common in the Bible. In those ancient languages the names of cities were feminine. It should come as no surprise then that Babylon will be painted for us as the most evil of alluring "women of the night."

II. Babylon the Harlot (Rev 17:1–6)

"Then one of the seven angels who had the seven bowls came and said to me, 'Come, I will show you the judgment of the great whore who is seated on many waters, with whom the kings of the earth have committed fornication, and with the wine of whose fornication the inhabitants of the earth have become drunk.' So he carried me away in the spirit into a wilderness, and I saw a woman sitting on a scarlet beast that was full of blasphemous names, and it had seven heads and ten horns. The woman was clothed in purple and scarlet, and adorned with gold and jewels and pearls, holding in her hand a golden cup full of abominations and the impurities of her fornication; and on her forehead was written a name, a mystery: 'Babylon the great, mother of whores and of earth's abominations.' And I saw that the woman was drunk with the blood of the saints and the blood of the witnesses to Jesus" (Rev 17:1–6).

In sharp contrast to the heroic, valiant woman of Revelation 12:1, we now encounter her anti-type, the harlot. Whenever Jerusalem was unfaithful to her covenant with God, the prophets called the city a harlot (cf. Isa 1:21; 23:15–18). Now it is Babylon who is identified as the most evil temptress of history. She is clothed like the daughters of Sion (Isa 3:16–24). Her jewels jangle on her body (Ezek 28:11–16). Their sound announces her

The Great Harlot of Babylon (Rev 17)

occupation. Jeremiah spoke about Babylon as the cup from which the nations gladly imbibed, making them drunk (Jer 51:7). Now the harlot holds the cup filled with idolatrous vices and all the filth of sin. The picture stands in sharp contrast to the external beauty of the harlot's painted face.

She rides on the beast, like a conquering heroine. Her robes are scarlet, representing both the color of her business (Josh 2) and the color of the Roman imperial standard. Ancient Babylon and Rome were filled with buildings that inspired awe. Inscriptions on the buildings, still visible today in Rome, identified the function of the building. In contrast to those marked with the sign of salvation, this harlot announces her true identity as "mother of harlots and all the world's abominations." What appears beautiful at first glance is, in fact, filthy. So it is with most evil. It appears good; it seems attractive. Only later does it deal death (cf. Gen 3:6).

III. The Interpretation of the Vision (Rev 17:7–18)

We are advised that a certain amount of wisdom can help us interpret the vision (Rev 13:18; 17:9). The seven heads are seven hills, obviously the famous seven hills of Rome. Although the numbering gets a little confusing, the references are also to the historical emperors of Rome from the time of Jesus to the writing of Revelation. They were Augustus, Tiberius, Caligula, Claudius, Nero (Galba, Otho, Vitellius, whose reigns were very short), Vespasian, Titus, and Domitian, emperor at the time that Revelation was written. The emperors from Caligula on are figured in the number imagery that is used in these verses. Nero, as we already saw, was the source of many legends about dying and returning. He will figure as the eighth beast as well as the third. Vespasian was the military leader who began the siege and destruction of Jerusalem. His son Titus finished the deed. They were despised by both Jews and Christians. Domitian, who was on the throne when Revelation was written, was known to be neurotic. He even had his palace lined with mica in order to reflect the images of any would-be assassins.

The horns represent the other kings of the earth, probably the Parthian satraps of the east. God, who is Lord of History, can easily arrange for them to do the divine will. They will confer their considerable military might upon the beast, thus making the odds against the Lamb even greater. (In 1 Kgs 18 the prophet Elijah fought odds of 450 to 1.) But the Lamb will conquer. "They will make war on the Lamb, and the Lamb will conquer them, for he is the Lord of lords and King of kings, and those with him are called and chosen and faithful" (Rev 17:14). God's faithful ones are not deceived by the outward appearance of the harlot. They are able to distinguish right from wrong, truth from falsehood, good from evil. With the Lamb fighting for them, they will be victorious.

IV. The Doom of Babylon (Rev 18:1–24)

There are many songs in the Book of Revelation. We have already seen the songs of rejoicing that are chanted by the faithful in heaven. These were the songs of the angels, announcing the vindication of God. Now we hear a funeral lamentation sung over Babylon. The prophets liked to sing funeral songs about the future. By proclaiming a sorrowful future, it was as good as an accomplished fact. Thus the prophet Amos sings about Israel: "Hear this word that I take up over you in lamentation, O house of Israel: Fallen, no more to rise, is maiden Israel; forsaken on her land, with no one to raise her up" (Amos 5:1–2).

Isaiah 23 recounts a funeral song for Tyre, Sidon, and Tarshish, the great commercial empires of that era. Jeremiah 50–51 recounts oracles of destruction against the Babylon of the prophet's time. Ezekiel 26 also chants a song of ruin against Tyre. John is joining good company in his funeral song for "Babylon the Great." Thus sings the avenging angel: "Fallen, fallen is Babylon the great! It has become a dwelling place of demons, a haunt of every foul and hateful bird, a haunt of every foul and hateful beast. For all the nations have drunk of the wine of the wrath of her fornication, and the kings of the earth have committed fornication with her, and the merchants of the earth have grown rich from the power of her luxury" (Rev 18:2–3).

This is the verdict of the heavenly court. The people of God are warned to get out of this condemned city quickly, lest they suffer along with the unholy. There is a parallel to this in the story of the destruction of Sodom and Gomorrah in Genesis 18:16–19:29. In the song that announces the end of Babylon, all the plagues, which have been meted out a little at a time throughout Revelation, will be dumped upon her all at once. She who was a harlot queen will become a widow and childless. But there will be no mourning for her.

She will not suffer alone. Everyone who has made their fortune off her evil ways will also suffer. Kings, merchants, and seafarers are singled out for ruin. Following an easily memorized formula, their destruction is carried out programmatically:

1. "Alas, alas, great city…"
2. Kings lose their power, merchants their inventory, and seafarers their cargo. The devastation is complete. It is the end of political and economic tyranny.
3. The ruin will happen quickly—in a single hour.

The vengeance song, so strange to modern Christian ears, echoes through the whole cosmos. The song of Jeremiah against Babylon (Jer 51:63–64) comes true. The mighty angel picks up a large stone that represents the whole city and casts it into the sea, just as the stone representing Babylon was cast into the Euphrates River.

All the bloodshed of the prophets and saints is now avenged in the bloodguilt of Babylon. She is no more.

V. The Canticle of Joy in Heaven (Rev 19:1–10)

We are taken back to the divine throne room to share in the victory celebration. Three psalms, each beginning with *Halleluia!*, ring out in heaven. The cause for rejoicing is not only what has been, the destruction of Babylon/ Rome, but also over what is yet to be: the wedding feast of the Lamb. The eschatological era has been likened to a wedding elsewhere in the Bible (Matt 25:1–13; Luke 12:35–40; John 2:1–12). The bride, those who are faithful in suffering and dressed in the white of purity and victory, is the direct opposite of the harlot Babylon.

But once again, we are left on the edge of our seats. Babylon, the evil city has been destroyed, but the beast still roams the earth.

Questions for Reflection

1. Who mourns the destruction of the city before they themselves are destroyed? Why are these groups singled out?

2. What is the relationship among religion, politics, and economy in the ancient world? in our own times?

3. What pairs of opposites are found in this section?

4. Note the dualism here, that is, groups who are totally good versus groups that are totally bad. Is any in-between area possible?

5. List some modern cities and what they personify. Which have good reputations? Which ones have evil reputations?

Chapter 10

The Coming of Christ
(Rev 19:11–22:5)

I. Introduction

The warfare of this book seems never-ending. Images of violence and destruction continue to fill the pages of the Apocalypse. The mighty enemy, the entire cosmos of evil, will not yield without a valiant and final battle. This is the eternal message of mythology. The Book of Revelation knows the format well. It continues to keep us on the edge of our seats. Slowly but surely the various enemies of God's people are vanquished even though the odds were definitely against such an outcome. Of course, when it is God who fights the battle, God will win.

In this section of the Book of Revelation the final destruction of the powers of evil and chaos finally takes place. The saints will have cause to rejoice forever. Rome, that high-spirited, haughty opponent, exists no more. The petty tyrants and cheating merchants exist no more. Only the great beast and the false prophet are left. The story continues with the tale of their demise.

II. Victory of Christ over the Beast and the False Prophet (Rev 19:11–21)

The Messiah of Israel was a king, the Anointed One, chosen to lead Israel in battle against her enemies. As king after king in the history of Judah and Israel failed to accomplish their noble purpose, the theological notion of the Messiah became more and more romanticized and idealized. By the time of Jesus, messianic expectations were high. Someone would have to come and save the people from the misery of Roman occupation.

The image painted in Revelation 19:11–21 is that of the heavenly Messiah going out as a king for battle against the enemies of God. The truth, of course, is that Christ had actually already conquered these enemies by his cross and resurrection. John, however, portrays the battle in typical, apocalyptic, mythological, and very exciting words.

The messianic king enters the battle on a white horse. Victory is presumed. Justice is his standard. For the Jewish people, justice was one of the primary attributes of the proper living of day-to-day religion. It meant everyone got what was proper. A just person was the paragon of religious virtue (Mic 6:6). Could the Messiah be anything less? The many eyes represent his wisdom. The crowns on his head do not weigh this warrior down. Rather, they signal his sovereignty over all who would contest with him.

The angels and martyrs of heaven ride out to do battle with him, a mighty host! His sole weapon is a sharp sword, the eternal Word of God (Heb 4:12). The word of truth is a sufficient weapon against the kingdom of lies. His title as supreme commander is "King of kings and Lord of lords."

While the saints in heaven are preparing for the messianic banquet, the carrion-eating birds are feasting on the remains of the kings and knights who foolishly did not repent. The gruesome juxtaposition of these two meals is typical of apocalyptic. It is meant to be colorful, shocking, and dramatic. The flesh of these warriors will not even be accorded a proper burial, a great insult in the ancient mind.

The battle is not even described. It simply takes place. With unusual simplicity and paucity of words, John writes: "And the beast was captured, and with it the false prophet who had performed in its presence the signs by which he deceived those who had received the mark of the beast and those who worshiped its image. These two were thrown alive into the lake of fire that burns with sulfur" (Rev 19:20).

As the end of the book approaches, John begins to recapitulate its major themes: false prophet, the mark, worshiping the beast. The fiery pool of sulfur is the permanent state of Gehenna. Here, its pains are amplified by imagination. Eternal damnation is the punishment for those who fought against God, the anointed leader, and God's people.

III. The Thousand-Year Reign (Rev 20:1–6)

Such troubles this passage causes! Why couldn't the defeat of Satan have been more definitive? Why, again, the possibility of delay over the final inauguration of the kingdom?

Fundamentalists point to this verse with one hand and to the calendar with the other. Another millennium of Christianity was marked by the year 2000. Fundamentalists use this as a measuring rod of time for the beast. Will the beast then be released? As we have seen, such a reading is inconsistent with the imagery, style, and purpose of the book. A thousand years is a very long time. It is an especially long duration when compared to the "short time" that the beast will again be loose upon the earth. That is all the phrase means: a long time!

References to the first death speak about our natural human dying. The second death is the death of eternal damnation. Which is worse? What happened to those Christians who died before the Second Coming? Even by the end of the first Christian century, theological thinking about this topic was not very refined. A simple promise is given: those who remain faithful will share in the reign of Christ.

IV. Final Victory over Satan (Rev 20:7–10)

The final downfall of Satan is described briefly. No words are wasted. In the blink of an eye the thousand years pass and Satan once again prowls the earth. True to form, he musters an army to fight against God. In Revelation 12:13, sensing a possible victory, the dragon rose to fight again. Now it is Satan's turn to return to earth and make a last valiant effort to gain the world for the powers of evil.

Where do these warriors come from? Did some escape the "first final" destruction? Or have some of the dead been resuscitated for this venture? Gog and Magog are symbols of the pagan nation, borrowed from Ezekiel 38:1–39. Satan and the false prophet are tossed into the burning sulfur "forever and ever." The victory is finally complete!

V. The Final Judgment (Rev 20:11–15)

Again, the action moves quickly. The last judgment scene in Revelation has none of the grandeur of the scene in Matthew 25:31–46. It lacks the artistic strokes of Michelangelo's majestic fresco in the Sistine Chapel. It comes and goes quickly.

God is seated on the heavenly throne, looking very much like the Ancient One of Daniel 7:9. All the dead are assembled before God. They come from Sheol and from the sea. All graves are empty. The criterion for judgment is astonishingly simple: "And I saw the dead, great and small, standing before the throne, and books were opened. And the dead were judged according to their works, as recorded in the books" (Rev 20:12).

Conduct was the criterion. Fidelity to God's Word was the criterion. There was a certain performance principle. Those who had joined the forces of evil perished with evil. The others were already standing in the throne room of heaven. These good and faithful ones had been saved from all the bloody destruction. As a final coupe de grace death and the netherworld themselves were also tossed into the eternal pool of fire, never again to pester the saints. It is the fulfillment of St. Paul's victory shout over death: "Death has been swallowed up in victory" (1 Cor 15:54). St. Paul also boasts about the power of Jesus over death in these words: "The last enemy to be destroyed is death" (1 Cor 15:26).

VI. The New Creation (Rev 21:1–8)

New beginnings always excite us. They are occasions for hope and celebration. We celebrate the birth of babies. Every baby brings new hope into the world. We celebrate the New Year. Perhaps it will be better than the old.

There is a new beginning here, a new creation. The entire universe has been destroyed. The earth and sea, so

filled with evil in the old creation, exist no more. The age
of Noah has ended. After the Flood God had recreated the
earth, hoping it would be better than the first time. It
turned out to be no better. But now, the seer recognizes
that God is doing something new. In fact, only God, the
Creator, is able to do anything truly new. New is one of the
most important words in the Bible. When we come to
understand our relationship to God we are able to sing a
"new song" (Ps 96). God established a new relationship
with us, a new covenant (Jer 31:31ff.). Now God estab-
lishes a new heavens and a new earth. It is replete with a
New Jerusalem to replace the unfaithful Jerusalem of old.

"Then I saw a new heaven and a new earth; for the
first heaven and the first earth had passed away, and the
sea was no more. And I saw the holy city, the new
Jerusalem, coming down out of heaven from God, prepared as a bride adorned for her husband…" (Rev
21:1–2).

The visions of Isaiah (Isa 65:17) and Ezekiel (Ezek
37:27) have come to pass. The old creation, tired and
worn out, malfunctioning, is replaced by a new and dazzling creation. The loss of the sea was no great disaster.
Israel never liked it very much anyway. This new creation
is a proper dwelling place for the survivors, the redeemed,
who now share the eternal joy of the kingdom.

It is God who builds this new creation and New
Jerusalem. It is consecrated to God who is holy. Only that

which is holy can dwell within the confines of the city. There are no more wicked. Previously, the Presence of God in the city was the *Shekinah,* the symbol of God's Presence in the Holy of Holies of the Temple. Only the high priest was allowed to enter that part of the Temple and he could do it only once a year. Now the whole city was resplendent with the Presence of God. God is available to all people all the time.

This is the only place in the Book of Revelation where God speaks. The content of the words echoes the covenant promise at Sinai, a promise that was renewed through the prophets (Ezek 37:27). God is with the people. God truly is the Immanuel of Isaiah 7:14. God's own words reflect the richest theological traditions of Israel. What welcome and tender words they are, especially in the ears of a people whose lives have been torn by problems of overwhelming magnitude.

VII. The Heavenly Jerusalem (Rev 21:9–22:5)

"And in the spirit he carried me away to a great, high mountain and showed me the holy city Jerusalem coming down out of heaven from God. It has the glory of God and radiance like a very rare jewel, like jasper, clear as crystal. It has a great, high wall with twelve gates, and at the gates twelve angels, and on the gates are inscribed the names of the twelve tribes of the Israelites" (Rev 21:10–12).

Jerusalem. The holy city. It is sacred today to Jews, Christians, and Muslims. Jerusalem. Destroyed many times. Always rebuilt. It is the site of the Temple. Within its walls, Jesus preached. In this city he was condemned. From a borrowed grave, he rose. Jerusalem.

There is a legend that one does not come to Jerusalem for the first time. Jerusalem is always some-

The New Jerusalem (Rev 21:9–12)

where in us, perhaps in our hearts. There is another legend. It is a holy city and a place of joy. No one is allowed to be sad in Jerusalem. As pilgrims came to the city to celebrate the great festivals, they left their sorrows outside the gates. These jettisoned sorrows are the stones that surround the countryside.

Jerusalem. Its walls could be seen from a distance. Strong. Protective. Keeping danger out. Keeping holiness within. Stone walls. Massive walls. Today the wall built by Suleimann the Magnificent surrounds the Old City. It stands silently, watching the centuries go by. That wall was built in 1543. It still stands. It still witnesses violence. And joy. And hate. And love.

Seven gates lead into the city today. The New Gate. The Dung Gate. Herod's Gate. The Damascus Gate. Jaffa Gate. The Lion's Gate. Sion Gate. An eighth gate, the Golden Gate, no longer leads into the city. It was blocked up by the Muslims in medieval times when they learned that the Jews expected the Messiah to enter the city through it.

Courses of stone, one on top another. Jerusalem. A destiny. A promise. To the people of John's audience these words of the reconstruction of Jerusalem were a dream. Many of them still remembered the Jerusalem that the Romans had destroyed in 70 C.E. It was a scrap heap. A ruin. The splendid words of this New Jerusalem would have sent their hearts soaring, their imaginations reeling, their souls spinning. Jerusalem.

Could a city built by God be anything less? Note its dimensions. It no longer needs to skirt the hills and ravines. Its measurements are perfect. It is the exact opposite of the despised Babylon. Jerusalem continues to exist. Babylon is no more. Precious jewels are the building stones of Jerusalem, not rock. It has a perfect number of gates. Twelve. It has a perfect number of guards. Twelve. Perfect names. It is everything the prophets promised Jerusalem could be when its people would take seriously the path to holiness (Ezek 40:2, 5; 43:2–4; 48:31–35; Jer 30:18; Isa 26:1). What a splendid city the New Jerusalem is, a promise of God's presence to all people.

John continues to describe the attributes of this new dwelling place of God. "I saw no temple in the city, for its temple is the Lord God the Almighty and the Lamb. And the city has no need of sun or moon to shine on it, for the glory of God is its light, and its lamp is the Lamb" (Rev 21:22–25).

God has redone the work of Genesis. There is a new creation, consisting of a new heavens and a new earth. In those first biblical verses God is careful to separate light from darkness, sun from moon, moon from stars, and to assign each of them a proper role in creation.

It is only fitting that in this new creation God followed the original blueprint. However, in this creation there is no need of artificial light, for the light of the world now shines therein (John 9:5; 1 John 1:7). Isaiah's vision is coming true (Isa 60:1–20). Jerusalem needs no Temple. God is omnipresent. Because everyone within its walls is holy, there is no fear. The gates can remain open forever. Welcome pilgrims! All evil has been conquered. Isaiah's splendid vision of the true role of Jerusalem is finally a reality:

"In days to come the mountain of the LORD'S house shall be established as the highest of the mountains, and shall be raised above the hills; all the nations shall stream to it. Many peoples shall come and say, 'Come, let us go up to the mountain of the LORD, to the house of the God of Jacob; that he may teach us his ways and that we may walk in his paths.' For out of Zion shall go forth instruction, and the word of the LORD from Jerusalem. He shall judge between the nations, and shall arbitrate for many peoples; they shall beat their swords into plowshares, and their spears into pruning hooks; nation shall not lift up sword against nation, neither shall they learn war any more. O house of Jacob, come, let us walk in the light of the LORD!" (Isa 2:2–5).

The description of the New Jerusalem concludes with passages adapted from the vision of Ezekiel regarding the life-giving water. The real source of this life is true worship in an invigorated community of faith (Ezek 47). A new tree of life, unlike the tree in Genesis 2:9, provides abundant and tasty fruit.

VIII. Conclusion

Finally, the delays are over. Not only is evil conquered, but goodness now reigns supreme over all the earth. What God once declared "good" in Genesis is now not only good, but also holy. God has been true to the divine Word. The faithful have their reward—an eternity of life with God.

Questions for Reflection

1. Why do you think John doesn't go into detail when describing the great final battles?
2. Reread the letters to the churches. Are there any parallels in the passages on judgment?
3. Why is "newness" so important to us? Why does the "new" sometimes threaten us as well?
4. What are the categories of sinners that God mentions in the divine speech in Revelation 21:8?
5. Why is this vision of a New Jerusalem so important to John's audience?
6. Notice the way John is beginning to make a reprise of all his major themes.
7. In what way do "light" and "darkness" function as mythological themes? in Revelation? in Genesis? in our human psyches?

Chapter 11

The Conclusion of the Book of Revelation (Rev 22:6–21)

I. Introduction

We have reached the end of the revelations to the seer John. Typical of the apocalyptic form, the book concludes with a series of warnings about the truth and sacred nature of this revelation. John has not made it up. It is true. One had better pay attention or there will be bad consequences. John begins his summary this way: "And he said to me, 'These words are trustworthy and true, for the Lord, the God of the spirits of the prophets, has sent his angel to show his servants what must soon take place'" (Rev 22:6).

Near the end of this epilogue, John issues another caution to the listeners and warns them to deal carefully with this revelation: "I warn everyone who hears the words of the prophecy of this book: if anyone adds to them, God will add to that person the plagues described in

117

this book; if anyone takes away from the words of the book of this prophecy, God will take away that person's share in the tree of life and in the holy city, which are described in this book" (Rev 22:18–19). We have certainly been through too many trials and tribulations to want that to happen. The warning is well placed, and is a solemn reminder about the sacred nature of the Word of God.

As John winds down this incredible vision of the future, he quickly reviews all of the major themes that have permeated his message:

1. Angelic messengers accompany him throughout the journey into the eschatological future.
2. This is prophecy, a revelation of God's activity in the world.
3. "I am coming soon."
4. We are reminded of the holiness of God and the sacred nature of Jerusalem.
5. Jesus plays a central role in history.
6. Various titles for Jesus are reviewed.
7. To witness means not only to give testimony but also to be willing to give one's life.
8. The plagues of Exodus, revisited in Revelation, are once again mentioned.
9. All things can be divided into dualistic categories of good and evil, especially at the final judgment.
10. A beatitude, such as we saw at the beginning (Rev 1:3), is revisited now at the conclusion (Rev 22:14).

II. Final Warnings

John knew human nature well. Christian though they were, people were people and old vices could easily return unless everyone watched over her or his behavior. For that reason John issues these final warnings: "Let the evildoer still do evil, and the filthy still be filthy, and the righteous still do right, and the holy still be holy" (Rev 22:11). He also includes these somber words: "Outside are the dogs and sorcerers and fornicators and murderers and idolaters, and everyone who loves and practices falsehood" (Rev 22:15).

John inserts the phrase "I am coming soon!" three times in these few verses (Rev 22:7, 12, 20). In other verses he also mentions the proximity of the arrival of Jesus. John is fostering an Advent spirituality. Christians must always live in expectation of the imminent return of their Lord. If they do, their behavior will always be acceptable (Rev 22:12). They will be ready for judgment, with nothing to fear. They will always be holy, residing in the New Jerusalem. It is a proper spirituality for Christians. Early Christians, who were still pondering the delay of the Lord's Second Coming, perhaps found it easier to be attentive to such a warning. It is still good advice in our own time. Our yearly liturgical season of Advent reminds us of our basic posture before the Lord: remembering the ministry of Jesus in the past, celebrating his presence in our own times and communities, and hopefully expecting and eagerly anticipating the Coming of the Lord.

III. Conclusion

John's final words to us in this epilogue appear like a slide show. In word-pictures, one after another, he has taken us with him on his journey. Now, in the solemn liturgical language that so often appears throughout his message, we are transported into an early Christian assembly.

The gathering of the saints (Dan 7:9–14; Rev 7:1–14) is taking place. Only those who are holy, according to the standards we have met above, are allowed to be present. There, they offer their prayer. It is a prayer filled with hope and confidence from the lips and faith of the earliest Christian assemblies. St. Paul is the first to report its use in 1 Corinthians 16:22—*Maranatha.* It is an Aramaic prayer, the language of the people of Palestine at the time of Jesus. It can be understood in two ways: as *Marana-tha,* "Lord, come" ("Our Lord, Come"), an imperative; or as *Maran-atha,* "The Lord is coming." The word also appears in 1 Thessalonians 4:13–17 as a prayer for the quick return of the Lord.

In the context of the Book of Revelation the first reading is probably more appropriate—it is a fervent prayer for the Second Coming of the person of Jesus, the Lamb, the Perfect Witness, the Alpha and Omega of history.

The final words of the Book of Revelation and the final words of the Bible are simple and direct: "The grace of the Lord Jesus be with all the saints" (Rev 22:21).

The closing formula is typical of ancient letters. John began by telling us he was writing a letter. He has indeed done so. It is a glorious message, filled with symbolism and hope, offering consolation to those worried over their fate in this world and calling them in their time (and us in our time) to transcend fears and to live as the redeemed, chosen, beloved people of God.

The last word of the Book of Revelation and of the Bible is certainly appropriate: *Amen*.

Questions for Reflection

1. In what ways does John recapitulate all his themes in these final verses?

2. How would you explain the positive nature of this book to a friend?

3. Are you surprised by the ending? Why or why not?

4. In the end, is the Book of Revelation practical? How?

5. Why is the prayerful ending so appropriate?

6. Why is an "Advent spirituality" proper for Christians today?

7. How would you summarize the message of the Book of Revelation?

Chapter 12

The End or the Beginning?

Some years ago, I taught at Dominican High School in Whitefish Bay, Wisconsin. It was the early 1980s and the "evil empire" and fundamentalism were rampant. Students raised questions about faith, hope, fear, and the future. Their questions prompted a course on the Book of Revelation that comprises the beginning of this book.

Those questions and fears were not only their own. Believing people often live with a sense of dread over the future and fear of the unknown. In the months since this text was first submitted, terrorists attacked our nation, the infamous 11 September 2001 "Attack on America." The questions that people ask about those events are haunting echoes of other questions from the first generation of believers. How can such evil exist? How are Christians to respond to the reality of evil in our world? Where is God when such things happen? How do we deal with a gospel of forgiveness when revenge and retaliation seem so necessary? Some people still find answers in strange fundamentalist approaches: This has happened because God is angry and is punishing us.

The millennial year 2000 has come and gone. "Y2K" was a hollow threat. All the pronouncements that the world would end at the beginning of that year have proven false. Such thinking was based upon a poor understanding of theology and of apocalyptic thinking and literature. The aim of this book is to search through the text of Revelation and uncover the broader themes that address such eschatological topics. The Book of Revelation presumes some familiarity with those themes. In this book we surveyed the apocalyptic style of the author and the apocalyptic mood of the times.

There are two lessons to learn. The first is that any attempt to read the Book of Revelation and interpret its words as portents portraying specific future persons, places, or events is alien to the design of the author and to good Catholic exegesis. The second lesson is that the Book of Revelation, which is so often interpreted and preached in negative ways, is actually filled with hope for the future. This was the reason for the original course and the reason for this book. I wanted to help people understand the biblical message that the purpose of this world and the direction of human history originate with God and will culminate in God, a God who loves us.

Many fearful things happen in this world of ours. Despite those realities, over and over again the God of the

Bible says, "Be not afraid!" Fear can paralyze us. In the end, fear serves no purpose. On the other hand, confident hope in God can give us energy and direction. It keeps us balanced while we live in this real world. We live each day, make our decisions, and interact with one another and with God according to our basic outlook on life: either hope or fear. To many readers, the end described in the Book of Revelation implies only destruction. Revelation teaches that the "end," in fact, is a celebration of the glorious coming of God's reign. Such hope gives us the staying power we need when the awful evils of this world and the deeds of some of its people seem to be winning.

The Book of Revelation, like all the other books of the Bible, calls us to make choices. The choices between right and wrong, good and evil, aren't always clear. They can be painfully subtle. There are always those who will chose the apparent truth over real truth and convenience or control over real good. There are always those who are willing to give power to the beast. Institutions and persons can become diabolical. We saw that on 11 September 2001. On that same day we also saw the power of good as strangers risked their lives to help one another. What a demonstration of the power of good over evil!

The Bible always confronts us with this choice: which kingdom do we believe in? Whose word do we follow? The gospel and the truth are demanding. They demand allegiance to Christ and courageous public witness to that belief. They also provide the help we need to live with love and with justice. We see glimpses of God's kingdom in our world, in our church, in our parishes, in our families — even in ourselves. Our baptism does mark us out as different. Each day our wise, faithful, and hopeful choices sprinkle a little more baptismal water on us. Good choices and the staying power of faith impel us closer to the kingdom of God and also bring that kingdom closer to this fragile world of ours.

We believe that Jesus is our Lord. He is also our model. He speaks the Truth. We join with those early, courageous Christians and with other Christians throughout the ages who have awaited the glorious return of Jesus, and we offer their simple, fervent prayer: *"Maranatha! Come, Lord Jesus!"* May our waiting be hopeful and holy.

Epilogue

Knowing Your Bible

The special place of the Book of Revelation in the context of the whole Bible can be best understood if the reader has an idea of how the whole Bible was formed, how it was written, how it was put together. The Book of Revelation presumes the reader is familiar with many diverse elements of the Bible and with how the Bible was written. Here is a summary of those important pieces of the background that serves as the stage for the Book of Revelation.

Many of the writings of the Hebrew Bible were preserved like an archaeological site. Just as the strata of a tel can reveal something about the crisis, catastrophe, and rebirth of an ancient city, in the same way the writings of the Scriptures can help us read the life of ancient faith communities. Their experiences were put into writing not only to help them understand what was happening in their midst, but also so that at another time, in another place, another community may forestall its own crisis or learn how to weather it with faith.

It was the fall of Jerusalem to the Babylonians in 587 B.C.E. that brought about the first real scrolls of the Bible

(Old Testament) as we know them. At that time synagogues replaced the Jerusalem Temple. These synagogues were a new invention, places where people could hear their history, their story, and lean about God's activity on their behalf. Originally the term referred to the gathering of the poeple, rather than to the building itself.

I. The Old Testament (The Hebrew Bible)

The first encounters of people and God are recorded in the Old Testament (the Hebrew Bible). There are three divisions to the Hebrew Bible: the Torah, the Prophets, and the Writings.

A. Torah: The Torah is the heart of Judaism. In these first five books (Genesis, Exodus, Leviticus, Numbers, Deuteronomy) Israel reports its experience of God. The Torah is often referred to by its Greek name, *Pentateuch,* meaning "five volumes." It is not a collection of books, but a single work comprised of five parts. It is also referred to as the "Five Books of Moses." In these books we read about the marvelous way in which a chosen people is called out of slavery and into life in a Promised Land with a special covenant with God, whose name is Yahweh or Adonai.

The Torah actually begins with the story of the freedom of the Hebrew people after a life of slavery in Egypt. This is found in the Book of Exodus. The foundation of their faith was laid by Moses in the desert. There they experienced God as a God of compassion and promise. The writings of the Torah were composed over many centuries. The laws and practices of different periods of time are found within the pages of the Torah. According to Jewish teaching, all five books are permeated by the spirit of Moses although we know he did not actually write the words.

Within these five books scholars have charted four different strands of tradition. The earliest is called the *J* or *Jahwist* source. We know that it originated in the southern kingdom of Judah, particularly in the capital, Jerusalem, and was probably written around 950 B.C.E. The anonymous Jahwist author is the first person to attempt an overall theology of the Hebrew experience of God. Through his writings, we view Israel at the time that this people is beginning to enter world history and to produce its story in literature. The Jahwist portrays God's constant concern for creation, a depth of feeling, and the tragedy that sin and self-assertion can bring to a relationship with God. God seeks to liberate creation from sin. The Jahwist has a reputation as a storyteller. He is particularly notable for employing the sacred name of God, *YHWH*, when referring to the Divinity, hence the title "Jahwist."

The second source is the *E* or *Elohist*. This author uses *Elohim* as the name of God. This tradition developed more in the northern kingdom (Israel). Writing around 850 B.C.E., the author records the history of the people from the time of the patriarchs through the wilderness trek of the Hebrews. In this E source, God often speaks through messengers (angels). There is a great concern for strict morality and the central orthodoxy of the all-important Sinai covenant.

The third source is the *D* or *Deuteronomic* source. It was written around 650 B.C.E. and became the backbone of the great religious reform movement of King Josiah. The purpose of this reform was to try to recapture the spirit of Moses, his teachings, and the ancient covenant for the times in which the author was living. It stresses that Israel must remain faithful to the covenant or the people will perish. Attentive obedience to the Word of God (especially in the prophets) will guarantee blessing. Apostasy brings disaster. The author writes in an emphatic style of lengthy sermons as though they come from the lips of Moses himself. The Book of Deuteronomy comes from this source.

The last source is the *P* or *Priestly* source. It is characterized by the typical concerns that priests would have for cultic matters and religious laws. Its style is precise, detailed, factual, and well organized. The Priestly author hammers out a hard-line monotheism. In reality it took centuries of experience to develop that monotheistic viewpoint that we take for granted. For this author, God is transcendent and exalted. God calls people to approach the divine through a series of covenants, the greatest of which was made at Mount Sinai, where Israel first became a worshiping community. The Priestly Source is generally dated around 550–450 B.C.E.

The central concern of the Torah is to explain the initial dealings of God with the chosen people, Israel. The Exodus from Egypt and the covenant that God made with the people in the wilderness of Sinai (Exod 2–24) is its heart. All else in Israel's subsequent experience will be measured against these books.

The Book of Revelation borrows heavily from both Genesis and Exodus. All the passages dealing with the destruction of the world in the Book of Revelation are the opposite of the creation accounts we read in Genesis 1–2. Likewise, the Book of Exodus and the narration of the plagues against Egypt form a major portion of the destructive sections of the Book of Revelation. John deliberately employed these images that would have been familiar to his audience.

B. The Prophets: Where do prophets come from? They are raised up by God. Who are the prophets? They are people like everyone else. What is so unique about the prophets of Israel? In situation after situation, the prophets stood up to speak the Word of God to a people who were forever forsaking the covenant. Without the prophets, Israel's faith would not have survived.

The term *prophet* comes from a Greek word that means "one who speaks for another," especially one who speaks for a god. The Hebrew Bible uses the word *nabi*. This means "one who communicates the divine will, one who is spoken to by God." The prophet is not a fortuneteller or a predictor of the distant future. Prophetic concern is always the immediate future and a summons to people to be faithful to God within that context. The prophet is one who is sent with a message that belongs to someone else. It belongs to God.

The prophets wished to be effective. They were very familiar with the Hebrew notion of the power of the spoken word *(dabar)*. They were able to use words with a vigor and strength that touched people's lives. Even though people did not usually like what they heard, there was no way they could ignore the word of the prophet. The constant concern of the prophets was the covenant. It was their mission to awaken in people, both individually and especially communally, a concern for the questions of proper justice and worship that were at the heart of the ancient covenant.

In Christian Bibles there are sixteen books of the prophets. Four are called major books and twelve are minor books. The four Major Prophets are Isaiah, Jeremiah, Ezekiel, and Daniel. They are called major because these books are longer, not because they are more important.

There are three eras of prophecy in the Bible: early or ecstatic prophecy, classical prophecy, and postexilic prophecy. Early prophecy is characterized by groups of prophets who went about singing and dancing in a frenzy, then delivering oracles. Their words are not recorded in books that bear their names. A good example of such a prophet is Elijah (cf. 1 Kgs 17–19). The classical prophets warned Israel about the impending doom that would befall the people if the covenant was not strictly followed. The postexilic prophets mark the end of the prophetic tradition. Prophecy existed because there were kings. Once the era of independent kingship in Judah and Israel ended, prophecy was no longer needed. These prophets imitated the style of the classical prophets, but prophecy, as an institution in Israel, was coming to an end.

The prophetic understanding of history and God's activities in the affairs of people penetrates the Hebrew Bible and presents a whole outlook of life that helps us to understand the subject matter of the Apocalypse. Time after time in the Book of Revelation reference will be made to the prophets of ancient Israel. The prophets were able to speak their message in times of crisis and get inside people's hearts and stir them up as well as calm their fears.

C. The Writings: The third section of the Hebrew Bible is called the *Writings*. This section contains the various historical works that do not fall under the Torah or the Prophets. In these books the history of Israel is presented through a series of theological lenses. We also read here the way the sages such as Ecclesiastes interpreted everyday life. In the Hebrew Bible this section includes such books as Kings, Samuel, Psalms, and Proverbs. *Note:* There is a different order and a different number of books in this section in Jewish Bibles compared to Christian Bibles.

D. Summary: Together these three sections comprise the Hebrew Bible. There is a nickname used by the Jewish people to describe these books. That name is *TANAK*. It stands for the Hebrew abbreviation of the names of the books. *T* is the abbreviation for *Torah*. *N* is short for the prophets (in Hebrew, *Nebüm*). Finally, *K* is short for the Hebrew word *Ketubim,* which means "writings."

II. The New Testament (Christian Scriptures)

A. Introduction: The writings of the New Testament evoke familiar images for all of us. We think of the Gospels, the Epistles, and the other writings such as the Apocalypse or the Acts of the Apostles. In order to understand the nature of these New Testament writings it is helpful to understand the events that affected their composition.

In New Testament times the reality of the cross moved Christians to explain the mystery of a crucified Messiah. As the growing communities faced new problems, both theological and practical, they needed guidelines. Many of the early Christians were converts from Judaism. They recognized the pattern of crisis that had characterized the relationship of God to the people in the past. St. Paul expressed it this way: "For whatever was written in former days was written for our instruction, so that by steadfastness and by the encouragement of the scriptures we might have hope" (Rom 15:4).

There was no greater crisis in the lives of the first followers of Jesus than the cross. When Jesus died on the cross, people lost hope. Yet, at Pentecost, fifty days later, the apostles would announce that the cross was the unique passage to a hope for which all the writings produced by other crises had provided the plan and the pattern. Followers of Jesus soon recognized that the lives of disciples would not be above that of the Master. He suffered. So would they. To believe and attach oneself to a crucified Christ was to be drawn into his ministry, his trial, his cross, and, ultimately, his resurrection. The first response to this proclamation was ridicule and persecution. Out of the preaching of the early church about the life, death, and resurrection of Jesus came the desire and need for more knowledge about him. This knowledge took the form of literature—the New Testament.

The very first writings of the New Testament are the Pauline Epistles. It was St. Paul who spoke about the *meaning* of the life of Jesus, not his biography. His letters and his preaching began to produce the Sunday gathering of Christians we now call the church. No longer able to follow the prescriptions of the Torah because Jerusalem had been destroyed in 70 C.E. and because their conversion had cut them off from their families and communities, Christian converts from Judaism gathered to hear the good news—the message of Jesus. Gentile converts did the same.

Another human event led to the need for these written accounts. During the first Christian generation, from 30 C.E. to 60 C.E., there were still people who had seen and heard Jesus in person. With the end of that generation came the end of the eyewitnesses. To this mix, add the secular crises of Roman imperialism and Jewish resistance to it. Christians were considered to be apostates from Judaism. It was out of all this turmoil that the documents we call the New Testament began to emerge.

B. Epistles: The earliest writings are the Epistles. *Epistle* is from a Latin word meaning simply "letter." Of the twenty-seven New Testament books, twenty-one are letters. No books of the Old Testament are called letters. These letters reflect the influence of the Hellenistic world and the impact of Paul, the preacher. Although epistle writing was a very ancient practice, it was especially popular at the time of Paul.

The letters follow a general pattern or form. New Testament letters give evidence of these four elements. *1. Opening Formula:* It states who is writing the letter, to whom it is written, and a few words of greeting. Take a look at 2 Corinthians 1 or Philippians 1 or Galatians 1 for a typical example. Often in his opening paragraph Paul will summarize all the good things that have come about because of a particular community's belief in the Lordship of Jesus. *2. Thanksgiving:* In these few statements Paul or the authors of the other epistles focus on a basic theme. For example, in the letter to the Galatians, Paul expresses anger. In 2 Corinthians he writes about his desire to establish reconciliation in this divided community. *3. The Message Itself:* This forms the third and major section of an epistle. Generally, it contains doctrinal information, some truth of the Christian message, or ethical sermons exhorting a community to live according to good Christian conduct. *4. Conclusion and Final Greeting:* In the final paragraph the letters summarize some personal news or gossip, provide some instruction to an individual or two in the community, and then close with a blessing.

C. The Gospels: Sunday after Sunday Christian people around the world stand for the reading of the Gospel. The Gospel is the good news, the news that everyone has been waiting for. It is the news of salvation, an announcement of freedom from sin. This was the good news that announced the birth of a son to a king. This was the good news that runners brought to city after city—news that an enemy had fallen and now they were safe. This is the good news that was to be shouted from the mountaintops many generations before satellite communication and cell phones.

Like the Epistles, the Gospels were written in response to the needs of people to learn more about Jesus.

Each of the four Gospels gives us a very different portrait of Jesus. It is as if you were to sit in front of four different artists and have your picture drawn. Each would see you in a different way, emphasizing the qualities of your person that each artist uniquely perceives. The portraits of Jesus vary because each of the evangelists saw Jesus through a different experience and wrote for a different community. Their questions varied from place to place and time to time. For example, Mark was writing to a community undergoing the first persecutions. Mark saw Jesus as a man who knew how to suffer. In an almost haunting manner, he portrays a suffering Jesus. He does this to offer encouragement to a community that was experiencing questions, doubts, and suffering.

Matthew wrote for a community of Jewish converts to Christianity. For them the questions of continuity and change affected the life of the community. Matthew portrays Jesus as a great teacher in the tradition of Moses. Jesus is a new teacher who brings the traditional Torah to fulfillment.

Luke wrote about the same time as Matthew, around 85 C.E. His Gospel was addressed to yet another community, one where Christianity was beginning to take missionary form and to reach Gentile audiences. In Luke's Gospel we meet a Jesus of compassion, a Jesus who has time for the little people, a Jesus who teaches about compassion. Luke emphasizes forgiveness and welcoming back those who had gone astray. He does this often by way of delightful parables. There is a special role for women in the Gospel of Luke.

These three Gospels are termed the "Synoptic Gospels" because they portray a somewhat similar picture of Jesus. The general outline of activity is parallel in these three Gospels. Make no mistake, though—there are significant theological differences among them

The Fourth Gospel tradition is that of John. For John, Jesus was from every moment of his existence the Son of God who was in complete control of everything he did and every situation around him. John wrote for a community that was also separated from its Jewish roots. He emphasized the superiority of Jesus over the old ways (replacement theology) and described the victory of Jesus over the darkness of the world. This Gospel was written in the 90s.

The Gospels were written only as a result of a long tradition of passing on the memories about Jesus. In any human experience we gather memories that are precious to us. We store them away in our minds. Sometimes they are very general memories, like a summer from our childhood. Other memories are sharper, focusing our attention upon events that made a difference in our lives—the day a parent died, or the day we started our first job. Most middle-aged Americans remember the day John F. Kennedy was assassinated—where they were, whom they were with, and so on. A younger audience today will remember similar things about when they heard of the attacks of September 11, 2001. These memories are passed on by word of mouth from generation to generation. Finally, they are written down in a final form.

The Gospels came into existence through a similar process. They began with real-life experiences of Jesus and his followers. The next step was the apostolic preaching, the way the followers of Jesus remembered the things he said and did. Only after a long process of handing on these memories by word of mouth did they begin to be gathered into orderly formats that finally became our written Gospels. These three steps are often referred to by their "official" theological names: The *Sitz im Leben Jesus* (Setting in the Life of Jesus), the *Sitz im Leben der Kirche* (setting in the life of the church-oral tradition), and the *Sitz im Leben in Evangelium* (setting in the text of the Gospel).

D. Other Writings: The other writings of the New Testament consist of the Acts of the Apostles, the Letter to the Hebrews, and the Book of Revelation (Apocalypse).

The Acts of the Apostles, written by Luke, is the sequel to the Gospel of Luke. In this book, the Spirit of God acted with power within the believing community. The good news of Jesus is taken from Jerusalem and spread throughout all the earth. The heroes of this book are the two great apostles Paul and Peter. In a sense, it could be called the "Gospel of the Spirit" because it shows the way that the Word of God, when preached with conviction, can change the face of the earth.

The Letter to the Hebrews is not so much a letter, like those of St. Paul, as it is a theological dissertation about the meaning of the sacrifice of Jesus compared to the Temple sacrifices of ancient Israel.

The Book of Revelation is the story of how a persecuted community can remain faithful to Jesus and in the end triumph against terrible odds and powerful enemies. It is the end of the world as described by theological imagination.

Summary: Each part of the Bible plays its own special role in teaching us about God and ourselves. From the Torah, we learn about the life of ancient Israel. We learn about its experiences and its customs. A careful reading of Genesis 1–2 and Exodus 1–24 helps us to understand the new insights that the author of the Book of Revelation brings to those well-known events.

From the prophets we learn the language of renewal and expectation as well as the consequences of not listening to God's Word. Their uncompromising demands for fidelity to God and decent treatment of neighbor echo throughout the Book of Revelation. The prophets, like the author of Revelation, had to stand before the government authorities of their day, authorities whose concerns were survival in power and prestige, not teaching God's way. It is no surprise that much of the Book of Revelation uses their example of steadfast resistance to what is expedient as a way to communicate the same message in a new time and place. The prophet Daniel, especially, figures in the imagery of the Book of Revelation. By understanding the problems that the book confronts, it is easier to see why the author of Revelation turns to its pages for imagery and direction.

The sections of the prophets, especially Daniel, that contain apocalyptic messages and images were part and parcel of the era in which most of the Bible was written. A sense of dependence upon God in the face of the lack of human leadership and power pervades those works.

The Wisdom tradition also finds its way into the Book of Revelation. John tells us that we are "blessed" if we listen to these words and take the message to heart. The end of the Book of Revelation recapitulates that wisdom with its solemn warning to take care not to change the words. How wary the scribes who copied that ancient text must have been.

The Book of Revelation begins with the letters to the seven churches. When you keep in mind the letter writing of St. Paul, you can see how the author of Revelation incorporates this form of writing into this complicated book. Throughout all of human history people have written letters, some privately and others to be circulated publicly. John writes this kind of public letter, knowing that word would spread about his blessings and condemnations of each community.

In the Book of Revelation, one of the titles assigned to Jesus is "Alpha and Omega," the first and last letters of the Greek alphabet. It is a poetic way of stating that Jesus encompasses all that exists, all time, all seasons, and all reality. Our Bible begins with Genesis, the story of the beginning of the world, of creation, and of humanity. Those who pieced the Bible together over the centuries saw the Book of Revelation as a proper conclusion to the whole story of what happened from that beginning of the world. In Revelation, that old order, so full of infidelity to God and mistreatment of neighbor, comes to an end. It is proper, then, that the last book of the Bible not only recapitulates that sad story, but that the revelation of God in the Sacred Scriptures ends with a new creation, a new beginning, a new opportunity to respond to God's initiatives in our world, in our history, and in our lives. As with all beginnings, it is a season of hope. It is a time of grace. We find ourselves in those times, in the dispensation of a new covenant, a new opportunity to respond to God with faith, with grace, and with love. How do you think we will do?

Questions for Reflection

1. What part (book) of the Bible is your favorite? Why?
2. What is the process by which the biblical books came into existence as we read them?

3. Using a table of contents, locate the various sections of biblical writings in your Bible.

4. What new terms and concepts have you learned from this review?

5. What crisis of your own life or in our world today is presently affecting or forming us as a Church? as a nation? your own life?

6. Why is the very human manner in which the Bible was written a threat to some people?

Roman Emperors and the Administration of Judea in the First Century C.E.

This is a list of the Roman emperors and their procurators or legates who were influential at the time of the ministry of Jesus and the formation of the New Testament.

IN JUDEA	DATES	IN ROME	DATES
		Emperors	
Herod the Great	37–4 B.C.E.	Augustus	31 B.C.E.–14 C.E.
Archelaus	4 B.C.E.–6 C.E.	Tiberius I	14 C.E.–37 C.E.
Roman Prefects	**6-44**		
Coponius	6–9 C.E.		
Marcus Ambibulus	9–12		
Annius Rufus	12–15		
Valerius Gratus	15–26		
Pontius Pilate	26–36		
Marcellus	36/37		
Marullus	37–41	Caligula	37–41 C.E.
(King) Agrippa I	41–44	Claudius I	41–54
Roman Procurators	**44–66**		
Cuspius Fadus	44–46		
Tiberius Julius Alexander	46–48		
Ventidius Cumanus	48–52		

Antonius Felix	52–60	Nero	54 – 68
Porcius Festus	60–62		
Albinus	62–64		
Gessius Florus	64–66		
Roman Legates	**66–135**	**Galba**	**68–69**
Sextus Vettulenus Cerialis	70	Otho	69
Sextus Lucilius Bassus	71–73	Vitellius	69
Lucius Flavius Silva	73–81	Vespasian	69–79
Cnaeus Pompeius Longinus	86	Titus	79–81
Sextus Hermetidius Campanus	93	Domitian	81–96
Atticus	100	Nerva	96–98
Caius Julius Quadratus Bassus	102–105	Trajan	98–117
Quintus Roscius Coelius Pompeuis Falco	105–107		
Tiberianus (?)	114		
Lusius Quitus	117		
Quintus Tineius Rufus	132		
Caius Quinctius Certus Publius Marcellus	dates uncertain (134–135?)		
Sextus Julius Severus	135		

Apocryphal and Apocalyptic

Apocalypse means "to reveal" or "to open up." The word *apocryphal* means just the opposite. It means "to hide" or "to make secret." Exactly why this term came to be used is shrouded in history. It might be because the apocryphal books were thought to have knowledge that was too esoteric for the common person to understand. In the study of the Bible there are a number of books that are called apocryphal. Catholics and Protestants use this term differently. Catholics use the term when they refer to books that were written in the general era of the biblical books we find in our Bible but that were never accepted by the Church as authoritative. Protestants use this term in reference to books that are in the Catholic Bible but which they have rejected. To make things more complicated, Catholics use the term *Deutero-canonical* when they write about these texts.* There is yet a third term you should know: *pseudepigrapha*. This term more properly refers to the non-biblical writings, the "hidden writings" that sound like biblical books but that are rejected by the

---

*The books of Tobit, Judith, Wisdom of Solomon, Sirach, Baruch, 1–2 Maccabees appear in Catholic Bibles. They were included in the Septuagint (LXX), the Greek translation of the Hebrew Bible.

Jewish, Protestant, and Catholic traditions as non-biblical and non-authoritative.

That does not mean that they are not important or not of interest to us. The reason it is important to know something about these books is twofold. On the one hand, even though they were never accepted as biblical books, they give a lot of insight into the popular mind-set of that era (200 B.C.E.–200 C.E.) when the role of apocalyptic was so important. They are called apocryphal because many of them claim to have secret revelations. As you have seen from our reading of the Book of Revelation, that was a style of writing and a way of thinking that was very important.

Every once in a while when someone learns about the existence of these books the Church gets accused of hiding them. It is as though there was some secret information there that could cancel out our true beliefs that are formed from the Bible. A similar kind of excitement was generated in 1947 with the discovery of the Dead Sea Scrolls. Many copies of the "Old Testament" were among those scrolls. What was particularly exciting was that there were other writings that helped to explain the teachings of this very unusual group of people. One of their famous documents, *The War Between the Sons of Light and the Sons of Darkness,* is apocalyptic in nature. From what you already know about apocalyptic, you can see mythological elements even in the title.

There are apocryphal writings from the Old Testament era as well as from the New. Several of them can be classified as apocalyptic, because they use the general techniques we have seen in the Book of Revelation and reflect the general mind-set of waiting for God to intervene definitively in history to assist "the good guys" and to vanquish all the others.

Some of the works that include apocalyptic writings from the Old Testament era follow. *1. The Books of Enoch.* This work narrates the story of the principal character, Enoch, who travels to the underworld, the earth, and the heavens (the threefold cosmos of the ancient world). In those journeys he "sees" the Coming of the Messiah (for Christians, the return of Jesus) and the judgment of the world. *2. The Testaments of the Twelve Patriarchs.* This book is written as though it is addressed to the sons of Jacob, the patriarchs of ancient Israel, and foresees the future of Israel. *3. The Sibylline Oracles.* One of the most famous mythological characters of ancient times was Sybil, a prophetess. The Greeks originated this prophetess and other cultures freely borrowed the work, changing it and adapting it to their own teachings. Both the ancient Jews and early Christians did the same. It contains predictions about the Messiah. *4. Books of Baruch.* This work also deals with the Coming of the Messiah, among other topics. *4. 4 Esdras.* This book, which is also called 2 Esdras, discusses the delay of the Coming of the Messiah. Like the Book of Revelation, it includes woes and animal imagery.

New Testament apocryphal works include several gospels (the Gospel of James, the Gospel of Thomas, the Gospel of Peter, the Gospel of Nicodemus, and others), various letters (Epistle of Abgar, Epistle to the Laodiceans, Epistle of the Apostles), other Acts (Acts of Paul, Acts of Peter, Acts of Andrew, Acts of James, Acts of Philip), and some apocalypses.

These apocalypses use the kinds of imagery we have seen in the Book of Revelation. Most of them were written quite late in the early Christian period. They include the Apocalypse of Paul, the Apocalypse of Peter, and the Apocalypse of Thomas. These writings of the early Christian era often include Gnostic philosophies, the idea that there is some secret knowledge about the past or future that is shared only by the initiates.

What is important to remember is that these books were never accepted by the community, either Jewish or Christian. Their contents, while fascinating, did not speak to the authentic experience of God or Jesus. Their main value is the kind of background information that they provide about the mentality of those turbulent times.

Glossary

Adonai: A Hebrew name for God. This word is commonly used as a substitute for the sacred name of God, Yahweh.

Apocalyptic: The term *apocalyptic* refers to a style of writing (also called a form) that uses extraordinary imagery (e.g., numbers, beasts, etc). It also refers to an outlook or viewpoint about the future that believes that a present situation is so filled with evil that it could only be altered by a radical intervention of God in history.

Apocryphal: This terms means "hidden" or secret. It refers to writings that are not a part of the Bible, but contain interesting information and ideas that help us to understand the mind-set of the early church.

B.C.E.: This acronym stands for "Before the Common Era." It corresponds to the traditional usage of B.C., "Before Christ."

Canonical: Books that are part of the Bible. There is a slightly different listing of these books in Catholic Bibles and Protestant Bibles.

C.E.: This acronym stands for "common Era," also known as A.D. (Anno Domini).

Chiliasm: This is a Greek term that is parallel to the Latin word *millennium*. It means "a thousand." It refers to the belief that there will be a thousand-year reign of good before a final battle takes place between good and evil.

Covenant: A covenant is a relationship, an agreement or a contract between two people or two groups, for example, nations. In the Bible it refers primarily to the covenant made between God and Israel at Mount Sinai. It can also refer to the covenant made between God and King David (2 Sam 7). The new covenant refers to passage in Jeremiah 31 and the Last Supper words of Jesus.

Deutero-canonical: Old Testament books that appear in the Catholic Bible but are not included in Protestant or Jewish Bibles.

Deuteronomic: This is the third source of the Torah. It is usually abbreviated with the letter *D*.

Dualism: Dualism refers to dividing entities into two easily recognizable units, for example, good and evil. The term is usually associated with theological or philosophical ideas. It is also a rather simplistic and artificial division with little nuance or subtlety.

Elohist: This is the second source of the Torah. It is abbreviated with the letter *E*.

Eschatology: This is the formal term in theological study for all research and ideas about the end of the world.

Eschaton: This term comes from the Greek and refers to the "final age" or end of the world.

Gehenna: Also written *Gehennah,* this is the valley south and west of Jerusalem where people offered human sacrifices to the pagan god Molech. Later it became the garbage dump of Jerusalem. Because of the fires that always burned in the refuse heap, it became an image of hell.

Gematria: The symbolic use of numbers in Jewish mysticism. It assigns a numeric value to the letters of the Hebrew alphabet.

Hellenistic: This refers to Greek culture, language, or religion.

Inclusion: This term refers to a writing technique that begins and ends a piece of literature with the same words or ideas.

Jahwist: This is the first written source of the Torah. It is abbreviated with the letter *J*.

Messianic banquet: In the Hebrew Scriptures, in a land where food was hard-earned and often scarce, this term becomes the symbol of the gracious bounty of God. It is a meal in which there will be plenty of the best to eat and drink for everyone.

Millennialism: This is the Latin form of the term *chiliasm* (cf. above).

Millennium: A thousand years.

Parousia: This Greek term means "presence" or "advent" and refers to the return of Jesus at the end of the world.

Pentateuch: This is the Greek term for the Torah, the first five books of the Hebrew Bible.

Priestly: This term refers to the last of the four sources of the Torah. It is abbreviated with the letter *P*.

Pseudepigrapha: "False writings." This term refers to those books which were written in the biblical era but were never included in the Bible. They include many apocalyptic elements.

Pseudonymity: This is the use of false names. The reason for such use is either to impress an audience or to give a piece of writing a special authority. It is also used when an author might want protection because the contents of her or his work will be controversial or subversive.

Shekinah: The presence of God in the Holy of Holies in the Jerusalem Temple.

Synoptic: This term refers to the Gospels of Matthew, Mark, and Luke. It means "with a similar viewpoint." The term is used because these three Gospels narrate many of the same events and words of Jesus even though the theological message in each has its own special characteristics. The Gospel of John is considerably different.

Tanak: This is the Jewish name for their Bible, what Christians call the Old Testament.

Tel: A tel is an archeological site, usually a mound arising out of the surrounding countryside. The mound-like appearance comes from the many levels of civilization that have been built upon each other at a single site.

Torah: The Torah is the first five books of the Bible (Genesis, Exodus, Leviticus, Numbers, and Deuteronomy). It forms the heart of Judaism (cf. Pentateuch).

Weltanschauung: This German word means "worldview." It refers to a whole outlook or philosophy of life.

YHWH: Also Yahweh or Jahweh, this is the sacred name for God in the Old Testament that was revealed to Moses (Exod 3:14).

Bibliography

Aune, D. E. *Prophecy in Early Christianity and the Ancient Mediterranean World*. Grand Rapids: Eerdmans, 1983.

Batto, Bernard F. *Slaying the Dragons: Mythmaking in the Biblical Tradition*. Louisville/Westminster: John Knox, 1992.

Beale, G. K. *The Book of Revelation: A Commentary on the Greek Text, The New International Greek Testament Commentary*. Grand Rapids: Eerdmans, 1999.

Bloom, Harold. *The Revelation of St. John the Divine*. New York: Chelsea House, 1988.

Boadt, Lawrence. *Reading the Old Testament, An Introduction*. New York: Paulist, 1984.

Brown, Raymond. *The Community of the Beloved Disciple; The Life, Loves and Hates of an Individual Church in New Testament Times*. New York: Paulist, 1979.

Chapman, C. T. *The Message of the Book of Revelation*. Collegeville: The Liturgical Press, 1995.

Charles, R. H. *The Apocrypha and Pseudepigrapha of the Old Testament in English*, 2 vols. New York: Oxford University Press, 1913.

Charlesworth, James, editor. *The Old Testament Pseudepigrapha: Apocalyptic Literature and Testaments*. New York: Doubleday, 1983.

Collins, Adela Yarbro. *The Combat Myth in the Book of Revelation*. Missoula: Scholars, 1976.

————. *The Apocalypse New Testament Message*, 22. Wilmington: Glazier, 1979.

155

————. *Crisis and Catharsis: The Power of the Apocalypse.* Philadelphia: Westminster, 1984.

Collins, John. *The Apocalyptic Imagination: An Introduction to the Jewish Matrix of Christianity.* New York: Crossroad, 1984.

————. *The Apocalyptic Vision of the Book of Daniel,* Harvard Semitic Monographs, 16. Missoula: Scholars, 1977.

————. *Daniel, With an Introduction to Apocalyptic Literature,* Forms of the Old Testament Literature, 20. Grand Rapids: Eerdmans, 1984.

Collins, John, & Fishbane, Michael (eds.). *Death, Ecstasy and Other Worldly Journeys.* Albany: State University of New York Press, 1995.

Court, John M. *Myth and History in the Book of Revelation.* London: SPCK, 1979.

Feuillet, A. *The Apocalypse.* New York: Alba House, 1964.

Ford, Josephine Massynberde. *Revelation, Anchor Bible.* vol. 38. Garden City: Doubleday, 1975.

Glasson, T. F. *The Revelation of John, The Cambridge Bible Commentary, New English Bible.* Cambridge: Cambridge University Press, 1965.

Hanson, Paul (ed.). *Visionaries and Their Apocalypses.* Philadelphia: Fortress, 1983.

Harrington, Wilfrid. *Revelation Sacra Pagina,* vol. 16. Collegeville: The Liturgical Press, 1993.

Hemer, Colin J. *The Letters to the Seven Churches of Asia in Their Local Setting.* Sheffield: Journal for the Study of the Old Testament, 1986.

Himmelfarb, Martha. *Tours of Hell: The Apocalyptic Form in Jewish and Christian Literature.* Philadelphia: Fortress, 1983.

Horsley R., and Hanson, John J. *Bandits, Prophets and Messiahs: Popular Movements at the Time of Jesus*. New York: Seabury, 1985.

Krodel, G.A. *Revelation*. Minneapolis: Augsburg, 1989.

Kummel, W. *Introduction to the New Testament*, rev. ed. Nashville: Abingdon, 1975.

Lacocque, André. *The Book of Daniel*. Atlanta: Scholars, 1979.

Malina, Bruce J. *On the Genre and Message of Revelation: Star Visions and Sky Journeys*. Peabody: Hendrickson, 1995.

Minear, Paul S. *I Saw a New Earth: An Introduction to the Vision of the Apocalypse*. Washington/Cleveland: Corpus, 1968.

————. *New Testament Apocalyptic: Interpreting Biblical Texts Series*. Nashville: Abingdon, 1981.

Mounge, Robert H. *The Book of Revelation Revised*. Grand Rapids: Eerdmans, 1979.

Murphy, Frederick J. *Fallen is Babylon: The Revelation to John, The New Testament in Context*. Harrisburg: Trinity Press International, 1998.

Plastaras, J. *The God of Exodus: The Theology of the Exodus Narratives*. Milwaukee: Bruce, 1966.

Price, S. R. F. *Rituals and Power: The Roman Imperial Cult in Asia Minor*. Cambridge: Cambridge University Press, 1984.

Rolloff, J. *The Revelation of John*. Minneapolis: Fortress, 1993.

Russell, D. S. *Apocalyptic: Ancient and Modern*. Philadelphia: Fortress, 1978.

Schüssler-Fiorenza, Elizabeth. *The Book of Revelation: Justice and Judgment*. Philadelphia: Fortress, 1985.

Sweet, J. P. M. *Revelation*. Philadelphia: Westminster, 1979.

Worth, Roland H., Jr. *Seven Cities of the Apocalypse and Greco-Asian Culture*. New York: Paulist, 1999.